JN055259

STRUCTURAL DESIGN MAP TOKYO

Supervised by Ken'ichi Kawaguchi, Toru Takeuchi

Index map

Kanegafuchi Sta.

313

6

308

60

Higashi-Mukojima Sta.

Arakawa River

449

C2

315

Uguisudani Sta.

Shin-Koiwa Sta.

o Park

P.102

Hikifune Sta.

Ueno Sta.

Sensō-ji

465

Oshiage Sta.

chimachi Sta.

Asakusa Sta.

Tokyo Skytree Sta.

Hirai Sta.

bara Sta.

476

P.103

Ryogoku Sta.

Kinshichō Sta.

14

1

Asakusabashi Sta.

Kameido Sta.

7

Sumida River

nom-bashi Sta.

450

449

C2

Koto City Goverment Office

9

Etchūjima Sta.

453

Harumi Triton Square

319

Shiomi Sta.

P.12

P.128

Shin-Toyosu Sta.

Tokyo Aquatics Centre

P.13

P.129

Shin-kiba Sta.

Kasai-Rinkai-Koen Sta.

Shinonome Sta.

Kasai-Seaside-Park

P.126

Kokusai-tenjijō Sta.

7

daiba-nkōen Sta.

Tokyo Big Sight

elevision quarters ilding

Aomi Sta.

Telecom Center Sta.

Wakasu-Seaside-Park

0   1km

Preface

Ken'ichi Kawaguchi

Institute Of Industrial Science (II S)   Professor at The University of Tokyo

Megacity, Tokyo. Ever-developing international city of today.
It has more than four hundred years' history.
Since Samurai period, passing through the Meiji Restoration.

Due to its geographic location, the city and buildings are required the most
advanced structural technologies to prepare for various natural disasters such
as earthquakes or typhoons. Therefore, Tokyo is like a museum of the most
advanced construction technologies at the time. The structural design in Tokyo
is not just a smart cooperation of architects and structural engineers in general
sense. It is firmly backed by inevitable requirement for the highest safety.
The special effort of architects and engineers for the structural design makes
Tokyo the uniquely safest city in the world.

This book is an English digest version of the Japanese book published in 2014.

But it further contains additional parts of newly built facilities for Olympic and
Paralympic games 2020. There are so many interesting destinations in Tokyo.
We hope this book gives the most unique architectural guides to Tokyo strollers.

Toru Takeuchi

Structural Engineer,   Professor at Tokyo Institute of Technology

In Japan, the term "structural design" includes the concept of creative design
going beyond mere calculation according to design standards. This is due to
the fact that, while influenced by architectural and engineering education in
Europe and US, the peculiarities of structural engineering education, which was
derived from but integrated with architectural design in the wake of the 1923
Great Kanto Earthquake, and the conditions under which architectural design
must be carried out while enduring severe earthquakes, typhoons, and snow
accumulation, have made it difficult to realize creative design without in unison
with structural engineering.

This book is published as compact English version from the Japanese edition
published in 2014, with about 30 works carefully selected from original 140
especially for visitors to Tokyo city adding brand-new buildings. We hope you
will enjoy the structural design of Japanese architectural masterpieces in Tokyo.

Contents

How to use this book

This book picks up and introduces architectural works in and around Tokyo from structural point of views.

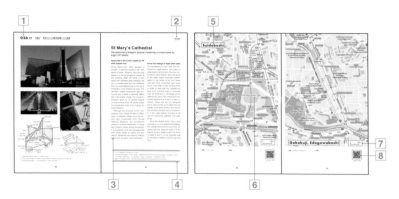

1. Thumb index

A number indicated at the top left of the first page of each architecture is used as reference in the map. Names of the prefecture, ward and name of the architecture in Japanese follow.

2. Keyword

Key words most related to the structural design of the architecture are indicated.

3. Text

Mainly explains structural design of the architecture. For non-professionals and beginners to enjoy reading, it describes the outline and structural features in the first half and more technical details in the second half. Illustrations and photographs are laid out in the same page for your better understanding.

4. Data

Following information is indicated: Address (In principle, street address is listed but the address of an item with high privacy such as a private resident is not listed.)/ Architectural design (Name of the architect or their firm is listed.)/ Structural design (Name of the structural designer or their firm is listed.)/ Construction (Name of the builder is listed.)/ The year of completion/ Structural type (classified by structural material).

5. Map name

The name of area mainly covered in the map.

6. Name of the architecture in the book

Architectures introduced in the book are colored pale red in the map.

Their names are typed in red. Index number, name and page in the book of the architecture are listed in this order.

7. Scale / orientation

Most of maps in Tokyo are scaled of 1/8000. For other maps, the scale is differed according to the usability. Orientation in each page is laid out so that the north is on top of the page.

8. QR code linked to Google Map

A google map with plots of architectures in the book is linked by QR code printed in the map.

*You might not be able to brows unless you have a Google account.
* If Google's service is not available, you will not be able to view the map.

Chapter 1

Olympic & Paralympic 2020-related venue

Japan National Stadium
Tokyo Aquatics Centre
Ariake Gymnastics Centre
Ariake Arena

Shinjuku Gyoen National Garden

Keio University School of Medicine

← To Shinjuku Sta.

Shinjuku Gyoen Nat's Garden-S.

Yotsuya Dairoku Elementary School

Keio University Hospital

Gaien Higashi-dori

Sendagaya Sta.

Gaiembashi

Chuo Line

Tsuda University

Gaien Entrance

Kokuritsu-Kyogijo Sta.

Gaien

A3

Tokyo Metropolitan Gymnasium

A2

A1

Gaien Brdg.

Tokyo Gymnasium Sub Arena

Meiji Memorial Picture Gallery

Tokyo Gymnasium

Tokyo Gymnasium Athletics stadium

Tokyo Gymnasium Indoor Swimming Pool

001 Japan National Stadium P.14

Tokyo Met. Gym

Meiji Jingu Park.

Gaien Nishi-dori

Meiji Park

Senjuin Temple

Meiji Jingu Stadium

Kasumigaoka Danchi

Kokugakuin High School

Aoyama High School

Prince Chichibu Memorial Rugby Stadium

Jingumae 3

418

Akasaka Fire Sta. Ent.

4a

Kita Street

4b

Watarium Art Museum →

2a

3

Gaienmae Sta.

1b

Gaien

1a

Harajuku Kindergarten

Aoyama Elementary School

Sendagaya, Gaienmae

MinamiAoyama 3

Gaien Nishi-dori

To Shibuya Sta.

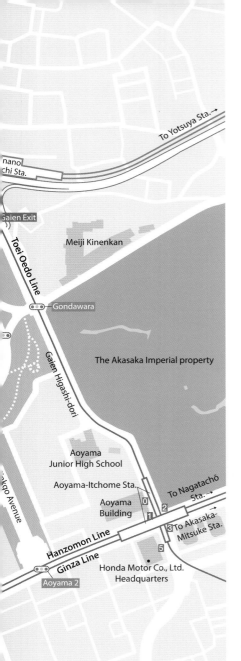

To Yotsuya Sta.→

nano
chi Sta.

Gaien Exit

Meiji Kinenkan

Toei Oedo Line

Gondawara

The Akasaka Imperial property

Gaien Higashi-dori

Aoyama
Junior High School

Aoyama-Itchome Sta.

kgo Avenue

Aoyama
Building

0

2

To Nagatachō
Sta. ←

3 To Akasaka-
Mitsuke Sta.

1

Hanzomon Line

5

Ginza Line

Aoyama 2

Honda Motor Co., Ltd.
Headquarters

319

Akasaka
Fire Station

Aoyama Cemetery

0   100m

001 Japan National Stadium   **P.14**

10-1 Kasumigaokamachi, Shinjuku-ku, Tokyo

google map

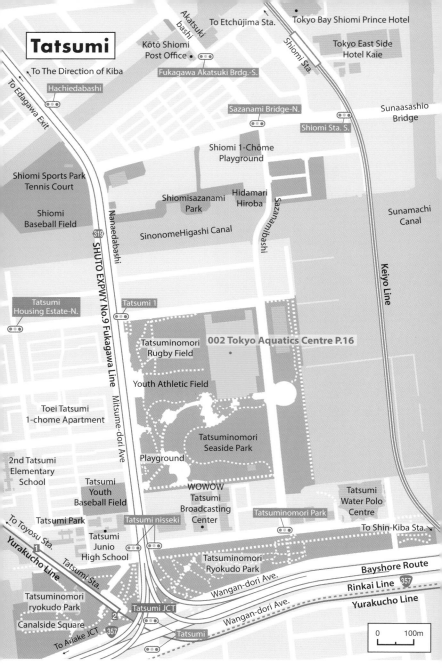

Tatsumi

To The Direction of Kiba →

Akatsuki bashi

To Etchūjima Sta. →

Tokyo Bay Shiomi Prince Hotel

Tokyo East Side Hotel Kaie

Kōtō Shiomi Post Office

Fukagawa Akatsuki Brdg.-S.

Hachiedabashi

To Edagawa Exit →

Sazanami Bridge-N.

Shiomi Sta.

Shiomi Sta. S.

Sunaasashio Bridge

Shiomi 1-Chōme Playground

Shiomi Sports Park Tennis Court

Shiomisazanami Park

Hidamari Hiroba

Sunamachi Canal

Shiomi Baseball Field

SinonomeHigashi Canal

Sazanamibashi

319

Nanaedabashi

SHUTO EXPWY No.9 Fukagawa Line

Keiyo Line

Tatsumi Housing Estate-N.

Tatsumi 1

002 Tokyo Aquatics Centre P.16

Tatsuminomori Rugby Field

Youth Athletic Field

Mitsume-dori Ave.

Toei Tatsumi 1-chome Apartment

Tatsuminomori Seaside Park

2nd Tatsumi Elementary School

Playground

Tatsumi Youth Baseball Field

WOWOW Tatsumi Broadcasting Center

Tatsuminomori Park

Tatsumi Water Polo Centre

Tatsumi Park

Tatsumi nisseki

To Shin-Kiba Sta. →

To Toyosu Sta. →

Yurakucho Line

1

Tatsumi Sta.

Tatsumi Junio High School

Tatsuminomori Ryokudo Park

Bayshore Route

Tatsuminomori ryokudo Park

2

Tatsumi JCT

Wangan-dori Ave.

Rinkai Line

357

Canalside Square

357

Tatsumi

Wangan-dori Ave.

Yurakucho Line

To Ariake JCT →

0   100m

---

002 Tokyo Aquatics Centre **P.16**

2-2-1 Tatsumi, Koto-Ku, Tokyo

google map

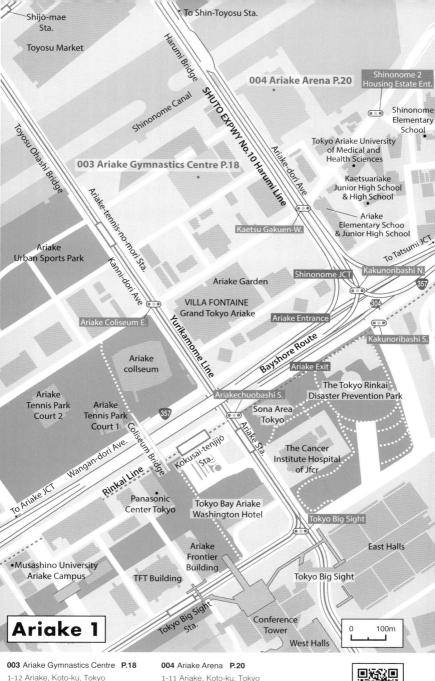

Shijō-mae Sta.

Toyosu Market

To Shin-Toyosu Sta.

004 Ariake Arena P.20

Shinonome 2 Housing Estate Ent.

Shinonome Elementary School

Harumi Bridge

Shinonome Canal

SHUTO EXPWY No.10 Harumi Line

Ariake-dori Ave

Tokyo Ariake University of Medical and Health Sciences

003 Ariake Gymnastics Centre P.18

Toyosu Ohashi Bridge

Kaetsuariake Junior High School & High School

Ariake Elementary Schoo & Junior High School

Kaetsu Gakuen-W.

Ariake-tennis-no-mori Sta.

Ariake Urban Sports Park

To Tatsumi JCT

Shinonome JCT

Kakunoribashi N.

357

304

Ariake Garden

Kanni-dori Ave

VILLA FONTAINE Grand Tokyo Ariake

Ariake Entrance

Ariake Coliseum E.

Yurikamome Line

Kakunoribashi S.

Bayshore Route

Ariake collseum

Ariake Exit

The Tokyo Rinkai Disaster Prevention Park

Ariake Tennis Park Court 2

Ariake Tennis Park Court 1

357

Ariakechuobashi S.

Sona Area Tokyo

Ariake Sta.

Wangan-dori Ave.

Coliseum Bridge

Kokusai-tenjijō Sta.

The Cancer Institute Hospital of Jfcr

To Ariake JCT

Rinkai Line

Panasonic Center Tokyo

Tokyo Bay Ariake Washington Hotel

Tokyo Big Sight

•Musashino University Ariake Campus

TFT Building

Ariake Frontier Building

East Halls

Tokyo Big Sight

Ariake 1

Tokyo Big Sight Sta.

Conference Tower

West Halls

0   100m

003 Ariake Gymnastics Centre **P.18**
1-12 Ariake, Koto-ku, Tokyo

004 Ariake Arena **P.20**
1-11 Ariake, Koto-ku, Tokyo

google map

13

1 / Aerial view from southeast
2 / Inside view
3 / Structure Overview

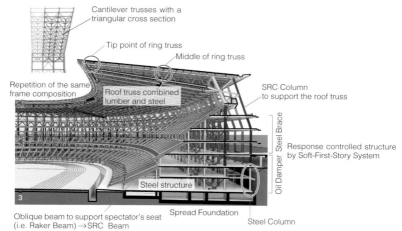

Cantilever trusses with a triangular cross section

Tip point of ring truss

Middle of ring truss

Repetition of the same frame composition

Roof truss combined lumber and steel

SRC Column to support the roof truss

Oil Damper　Steel Brace

Response controlled structure by Soft-First-Story System

Steel structure

Oblique beam to support spectator's seat (i.e. Raker Beam) →SRC Beam

Spread Foundation

Steel Column

Japan National Stadium
Simple frame considering constructability

Stadium in Forest

Japan National Stadium was newly constructed with the concept of "Stadium in Forest" in the historical and traditional environment of Outer Garden of Meiji Jingu Shrine.

The structure was designed with the theme of a disaster-resistant stadium, a world-class stadium using domestic lumber, and was planned with the highest priority on constructability.

Stand Structure

The main structure of the stadium is steel, and SRC members are adopted for the oblique beams (i.e. the raker beam) which support spectator seats, and for the outer columns which support the roof trusses. By employing the composition of same frames repeated in circumferential direction, by the precastization of the foundation and the SRC members, and by the proactive use of prefabrication products, productivity, transportability, the efficiency of drawings production and constructability were improved.

To increase resiliency of the stadium so that it can be used safely without being extensively repaired even after a huge earthquake. The response-controlled structure by Soft-First-Story

System using the lower three stories is effectively adopted. The lower three stories consisting of raker beams and braces are constructed to be less stiff than the upper stories by adopting a moment resisting frame using high-strength steel (550 N / mm^2 class), and oil dampers as a response control device. They are concentrically arranged all around in the lower three stories.

Roof Structure

The roof consists of cantilever trusses with a triangular cross section that are continuous in the circumferential direction. By designing the cantilever truss unit as a free-standing self-supporting structure, simultaneous construction of the stand, the field, and the roof portion was achieved.

Two ring trusses are arranged in the tip points and the middle part of cantilever trusses. These ring trusses integrate the roof frame and make it possible to resist against large disturbance as a whole.

The lower chords and the lattice members of the roof trusses are combined with lumber to prevent large deformation of the roof due to earthquakes or strong winds. Athletes and spectators can feel the warmth of wood.

10-1 Kasumigaokamachi, Shinjuku-ku, Tokyo

Design: Taisei Corporation, Azusa Sekkei Co., Ltd., and Kengo Kuma and Associates Joint Venture

Completion: 2019

Structure type: Spread foundation, Steel structure (partly SRC structure) for Stand, Steel structure (partly combined lumber) for Roof, Response-controlled structure by Soft-First-Story system

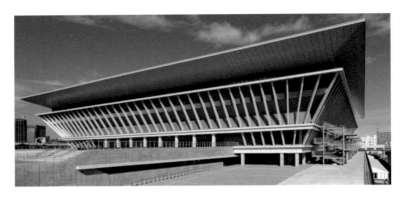

Raking slender column
Prestress concrete beam
Steel truss
Main arena
Sub arena

1

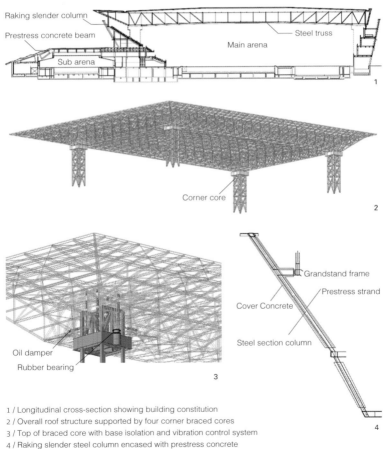

Corner core

2

Oil damper
Rubber bearing

3

Grandstand frame
Prestress strand
Cover Concrete
Steel section column

4

1 / Longitudinal cross-section showing building constitution
2 / Overall roof structure supported by four corner braced cores
3 / Top of braced core with base isolation and vibration control system
4 / Raking slender steel column encased with prestress concrete

Tokyo Aquatics Centre

Roof supported by four corner core that offer column free space and floating sense on façade

Outline

The Tokyo Aquatics Centre is the facilities newly developed by the Tokyo Metropolitan Government in the Tatsumi Seaside Park. This is a certified swimming facility equipped with a main pool, a sub pool and a diving pool in compliance with the international standards.

Main Arena Roof

The main arena roof spanning between corner cores offers column free space and floating sense on appearance. The roof is steel truss plate supported by two rubber bearings at each corner core to swap seismic input, and the oil and hysteresis dampers absorb input seismic energy. Each core also has vertical oil dampers to reduce vertical deflection at central part of the roof due to wind. These rubber bearings also work as buffer to absorb thermal extension and shrink to prevent onerous interaction force between the roof and corner cores.

Sub Arena Roof

The sub arena roof of prestress concrete beam gives enough stiffness to be used as approach to entrance, durability and dynamic view underneath. Each beam is precast dividing into seventeen units and assembled at construction site by tying prestress cables.

Perimeter Column

The perimeter column is slender steel column covered with prestressed concrete to prevent from buckling and satisfy with fire and rust resistance, inspiring traditional Japanese style. The upper part of the column is prestressed to reduce crack risk.

Roof Construction

The main arena roof was assembled at ground level, lifted up to its designed level, and set onto rubber bearings which were set so that its position fit to the roof deformation and take designed loadings.

2-2-1 Tatsumi, Koto-Ku, Tokyo
Schematic Design: YAMASHITA SEKKEI INC. / TANGE ASSOCIATES / Arup
Detail Design and Construction: Obayashi, Toko, Ergotech, Tonets JV
Completion: 2020
Building area: 28,245 m^2 / Overall floor area: 64,400 m^2 / Building height: 37 m
Structure type: Steel, composite at level 1, and partly concrete shear wall structure

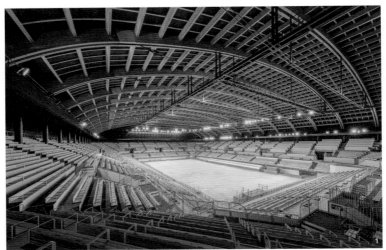

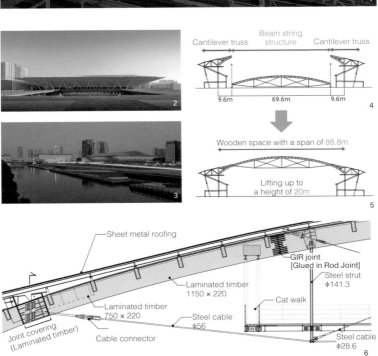

Cantilever truss   Beam string structure   Cantilever truss

9.6m   69.6m   9.6m

4

Wooden space with a span of 88.8m

Lifting up to a height of 20m

5

Sheet metal roofing

GIR joint [Glued in Rod Joint]

Steel strut φ141.3

Laminated timber 1150 × 220

Cat walk

Laminated timber 750 × 220

Steel cable φ56

Joint covering (Laminated timber)

Cable connector

Steel cable φ28.6

6

1 / Interior: Wooden space with a span of 88.8 m
2 / Exterior: Wooden vessel floating in the bay-area   3 / Night view
4–5 / Structural system of the roof   6 / Structural detail of the roof

Ariake Gymnastics Centre

A large space surrounded by wooden texture.

Wooden vessel floating in the bay-area.

This building was designed as a lightweight "wooden vessel" that embodies the memory of the site that was once a lumberyard and symbolizes Japanese wooden culture. The use of wood in this building is diverse, from exterior walls to the audience seating, and the roof structure .

Composite Beam-String Structure (BSS) for large woody spaces

The roof structure consists of three parts: cantilever trusses at both ends and a central Beam-String Structure (BSS). The cantilever trusses at both ends are 9.6 m long respectively and each BSS beams is 69.6 m long, and they are joined at to form composite beams with a span of 88.8 m. Timber is used for the upper chord of the BSS and the lower chord of the cantilever truss to optimize the strength of lumber against compression, and at the same time, the connected beam constitute a continuous arch. In order to avoid the combustion and sustain structural stability during a fire, glued laminated timber was used for its high heat capacity, rigidity and bearing strength under high-temperature conditions.

Sophisticated joint details emphasizing the beauty of wood

GIR joints (Glued in Rod=adhesive rebar insertion joints) are used for the joints between timber beams so that steel connecters are concealed from the outside view. The steel joints between the cables, steel tube struts and the timber beams are set in the gap between the pair of timber beams. The joint size between the cable and strut was reduced by using compressive joints. With these treatments, the timber beams create a simple and vivid arch shape on the roof.

Lift-up election realizing scaffold-free construction

The BSS, sub-beams, etc. are assembled at the ground level, and then lifted-up to a height of about 20 m and connected to the tips of the cantilever trusses. This enables to erect a large roof without scaffolding, while improving the efficiency, accuracy, and safety of the construction. The holistic design approach that encompasses techniques from design to dynamic construction demonstrates the high quality of Japanese construction technology.

1-12 Ariake, Koto-ku, Tokyo

Schematic design, Design development, Supervision for Construction documentation and Construction: NIKKEN SEKKEI

Design development, Construction documentation: Shimizu Corporation, Masao Saitoh (Engineering advisor)   Construction: Shimizu Corporation

Completion: 2019

Structure type: Steel, Timber (roof)

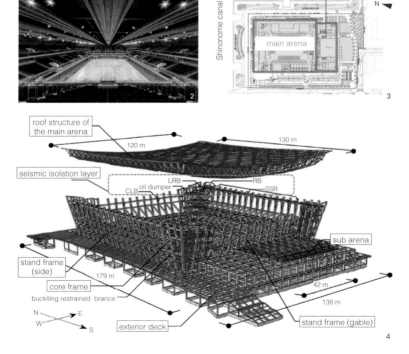

LRB: Lead plug-filled laminated Rubber Bearing
RB: Natural Rubber-based laminated Bearing
SSR: Low friction Sliding Support with Rubber-pad
CLB: Cross Linear Bearing

1/ Appearance from the canal side
2 / Inside of the main arena
3 / Floor plan of the building
4 / Structure diagram

Ariake Arena
Large arena roof with seismic isolation

Arena with seismically isolated roof

The arena was used as the venues for volleyball matches of Olympic and wheelchair basketball matches of Paralympic games during Tokyo2020. The arena elevation reflects the arena plan, which is wider at the roof level and gets narrower in the lower level, having inclined columns, to use the building area effectively.

The catenary shape of the large roof of 120 m × 130 m was designed to secure the necessary space inside and to control the height of the building in consideration of the surrounding environment. With this roof shape, the necessary structural dimensions can be secured, and the effect of reducing the air conditioning load can be expected by reducing the internal air volume to be air-conditioned. The roof is seismically isolated to secure high safety during major earthquakes.

Stand Frame and Core Frame

Since frames supporting the stand area have many repetitions, precast components are introduced as much as possible. Columns, inclined slightly, following the building design, have cantilever beams at their top to support the roof load, minimizing entire bending moment by reducing horizontal eccentricity of force lines from the bases of columns. Core frames at four corners are structurally designed with high rigidity and strength to take the major loadings of the building during earthquakes.

Roof Structures with Truss Girders

The roof structure is consisted of 22 main planar truss girders (120 m in length) and 7 planar bridging truss perpendicular to main girders. Lateral supporting beams parallel to the bridging trusses carry catwalks and serve as stiffeners of the main girders.

Seismic Isolation Scheme

Generally seismic isolation systems need boundary structures, for its recursive action and dumping reaction. The core frames are prepared with high rigidity in all direction for this function. LRB, RB and oil dumpers are mantled on the core frames and attached to the roof structure so that the core frames deal with the horizontal seismic load of the roof. Side stand frames and gable stand frames are equipped with SSR and CLB, respectively, so that they mainly bare the vertical load of the roof and reduce horizontal response.

1-11 Ariake, Koto-ku, Tokyo
Architectural design: Kume Sekkei (Basic design)+Takenaka (Final design)
Structural design: Kume Sekkei (Basic design)+Takenaka (Final design)
Engineering supervisor: Masao Saito   Construction: JV (Takenaka et al.)
Completion: 2019
Structure type: Roof Steel structure, Lower building S+RC+SRC

Chapter 2

Haneda Airport

Haneda Airport

005 Haneda Airport Terminal 2 **P.26**
3-4-2 Haneda Airport, Ota-ku, Tokyo

006 Haneda Airport Terminal 3 **P.28**
2-6-5 Haneda Airport, Ota-ku, Tokyo

google map

Airport North Tunnel

SHUTO EXPWY Bayshore Route
Wangan-dori Ave.
Wangan-dori Ave.

357

Haneda Airport

Tokyo International Airport Access Tunnel

Keikyu Airport Line

Haneda Airport
Terminal 3 Sta.

Tokyo Monorail

• 006 Haneda Airport Terminal 3 P.28

Haneda Airport
Terminal 3 Sta.

0   100m

Wangan-dori Ave.

Haneda Airport Exit

Haneda Airport Entrance

357

• 005 Haneda Airport Terminal 2 P.26

Haneda Airport Terminal 1・2 Sta.

Haneda Airport Terminal 2 Sta.

SHUTO EXPWY Bayshore Route

Haneda Airport Terminal 1 Sta.

Keikyu Airport Line

Airport South Tunnel

Wangan-dori Ave.

Shin-Seibijo Sta.

Tokyo Monorail

Wangan-Kanpachi

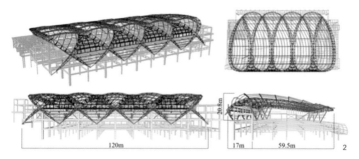

1/ Large opening on the apron side.

2/ Simulation model diagram of circle truss. The height of the structure was determined by required space for the chuck-in lobby and visibility from the control tower.

3/ A view during construction of circle truss and installation of ETFE cushions.

Haneda Airport Terminal 2
Three-dimensionally curved truss and inflated ETFE roof

Overview

The international flight terminal and its facilities were extensively built on the existing building for domestic flights. To reduce the additional load to the existing part, lightweight ETFE foils were used for the new large roof. Five sets of three-dimensionally curved circular frames with trusses are dynamically overlapping and shaping the new building and the roof.

The east side of the lobby faces toward the apron area, where aircraft can be observed. To make the most of this view, a wide opening with a glass façade, which connects the "sky" and "sea", was designed.

Circle truss

The large roof, 120 m × 62 m, is supported on the existing building with pin-bearings, not to transmit the bending moment to the existing part.

Each circle truss unit is 24 m-span and offset by half a span in plan and bent vertically, on one side, to form a curved surface that integrates the roof and wall surface. The upper and lower chords of the circle truss are made of φ400 mm steel pipe. The three-pronged pillars that support the roof, at the inside of the room, are made of tapered steel pipes with a diameter from 900 to 600 mm. The column base uses cast steel designed as a ball bearing.

Large opening

The circle trusses for the large opening facing the apron side are supported by V-shaped columns constructed outside of the room. The glass façade inside is reinforced by mullions hung from roof structure. The façade is designed to be looked as seamless as possible and realizes visually open space.

ETFE roof

318 pneumatic cushions, made of ETFE *1 foils, are used for the roof. Dimension of a cushion is about 3.5 m x 10 m in average. Each cushion has three layers, ETFE foils of 500μ, silver and white printed. for upper and lower layers while PTFE*2 membrane of 600μ, translucent, is used for middle inner layer. The middle layer is necessary to satisfy the non-combustibility of the roof, which is required by fire service act.

Normal inner pressure is about 300 Pa and is increased up to 600-1100 Pa in case of strong wind or snow fall.

*1 ETFE: Ethylene Tetra Fluoro Ethylene
*2 PTFE: Poly Tetra Fluoro Ethylene

3-4-2 Haneda Airport, Ota-ku, Tokyo
Architectural design: Azusa, Yasui, PCPJ, Tokyo International Terminal 2 International Facility Design Supervision Joint Venture   Structural design: Azusa, Yasui, PCPJ, Tokyo International Terminal 2 International Facility Design Supervision Joint Venture   Construction: Taisei Corporation   ETFE Cushion: Kyoritsu Industries Co. Ltd.   Structural type: Steel structure

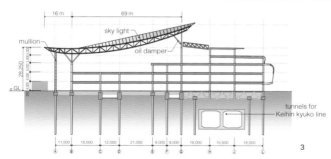

Haneda Airport Terminal 3

Vibration reduction in column-free open space

Airport with the image of the sky

Entering the departure lobby after passing through the airport access hall, a ceiling made of perforated metal floating like feathery cirrus clouds in the autumn sky can be seen. It rises higher as you move forward, and the passengers feel the openness of the departure area. The stage is a vast 15,000 m² column-free space.

Curved roof of large truss girder

The lower chord of the truss beam spanning 69 m draws a line with a large curvature that resembles a cirrus cloud. Having the upper chord as a compression element, flexural rigidity is secured. For such large span beams, vertical movement caused by earthquakes or strong winds cannot be ignored. In order to diminish vertical acceleration or deformation, an angle brace with a built-in damper is installed at one end of the truss beam to obtain damping effect. At the other end, cantilever beam extends 9 m from the truss beam and is connected to the glass façade.

Ingenuity for mullion

The mullion that structurally supports the large glass façade against wind load is a simple lattice structure. The mullion member connected to the roof is unbonded so that the axial force caused by the vertical movement of the large roof is not transmitted to the mullion. The unbonded member consists of a 60 mm diameter steel bar and is inserted into a 139.8 mm diameter steel pipe that prevents the bar from buckling. The 60 mm diameter steel bar restraints the vertical deformation of the cantilever beam.

By developing this structural system of the mullions, the open large roof structure has been realized.

1 / Exterior of the Terminal
2 / Truss beam with the image of a streak cloud
3 / Cross section

2-6-5 Haneda Airport, Ota-ku, Tokyo
Architectural Design:
Azusa / Yasui / PCRJ Haneda Airport International PTB Design Joint Venture
Structural Design: Haneda Airport International PTB Design Joint Venture
Construction: Kajima, Kitano, Toda, Konoike, Shimizu, Tokyu, Lotte JV
Completion: 2010
Structure type: Steel structure

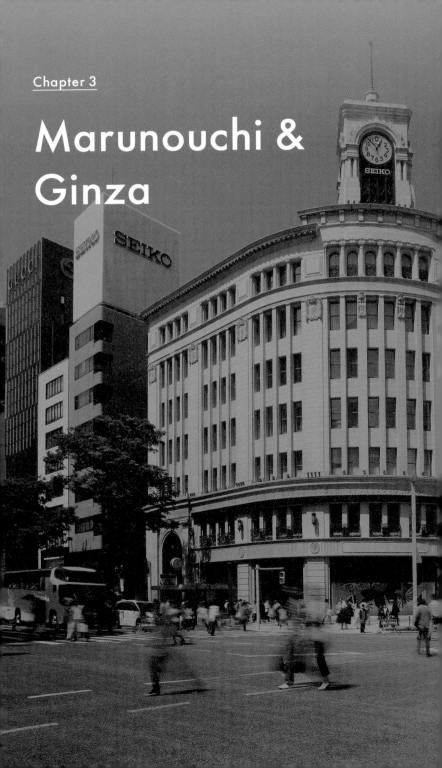

Marunouchi & Ginza

Marunouchi

google map

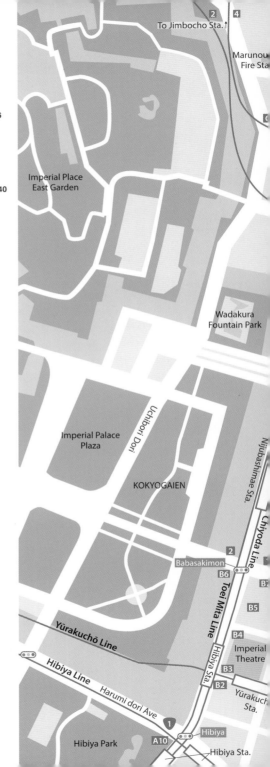

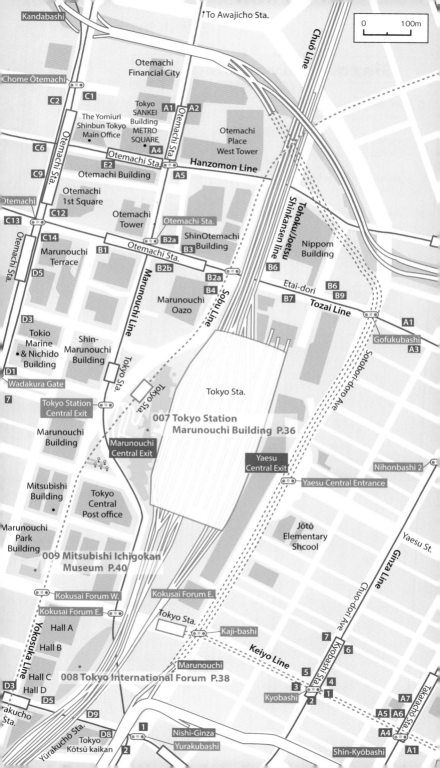

Ginza, Hibiya, Shimbashi

google map

1 / Overview of the renovated Tokyo Marunouchi Station Building

2–3 / The expansion joints between the building and its surroundings are the proofs of the seismic isolation structure. Let's think how it absorbs the differences in movement of not only at the floor level but also in the walls and ceilings.

4 / The wall surface of the original building is displayed on the concourse. Wooden bricks were fitted into the holes so that nails could be driven into the wall. A diagonal crack line due to uneven ground subsidence is also visible.

5 / Approximately 350 laminated rubber bearings (black shallow layer in the photo) and 160 oil dampers safely support the Marunouchi station building in the seismic isolation layer.

Tokyo Station
Marunouchi Station Building

Seismic isolation retrofit over 300 m long station

Restoration and Renovation of Marunouchi Station Building

Tokyo Station is the main entrance to Tokyo City. A major renovation of the station and redevelopment of surrounding areas were carried out for its Centennial in 2014.

The Marunouchi side of Tokyo Station is the original part which was built in 1914. A long and narrow majestic building with three stories, facing the Imperial Palace, has a length of 330 m and a width of 25 m. It was severely damaged in Tokyo air raids in May 1945, and more than 60 years had passed since it was reconstructed as a two-story building during an emergency treatment after the war. The building was decided to undergo large-scale renovation work, which lasted from 2007 to 2012. The restoration of the third floor and the dome roof were highlights of the works, which had been carried out while the building was kept functioning as a train station.

In the restoration of the Marunouchi station building, much consideration was taken to balance the revival of the original materials and construction schemes, with the addition of new functions.

Preservation: The existing brick walls with built-in steel frame were preserved as much as possible, while the brick walls taking higher stress were applied pre-stress in compression in vertical direction using PC steel stranded wires to improve the crack strength. Steel beams bent by fires were also reused or preserved in the original place.

Restoration plan: The structures on the third floor and the steeple were restored with SRC and RC structures, while, for the decorative ornaments of the dome, construction scheme and materials were selected to follow the originals as much as possible.

Seismic isolation structure plan: The existing steel-brick station building was supported by pine piles. Using the limited underground space, cast-in-place RC piles were newly installed to temporarily support the station building. Then the existing foundation was removed, two underground layers were newly built, and a seismic isolation layer was installed directly under the ground floor level.

1-9-1 Marunouchi, Chiyoda-ku, Tokyo
Original Architectural design: Kingo Tatsuno, Manji Kasai
Restoration and renovation design: East Japan Railway Company, JR East Design Corporation
Construction: Kajima Corporation, Shimizu Corporation, Tekken Corporation
Completion: 1914 (restoration and renovation 2012)
Structure type: Steel frame and brick, RC structure, SRC structure

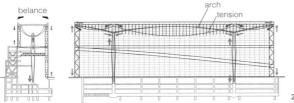

Tokyo International Forum

Keel-shaped glass and steel atrium supported by full-height columns

Structure centered around the keel shaped steel roof

The Tokyo International Forum is a major conference center located in the city-center that includes several exhibition halls and conference rooms. The central feature of this building is the keel-shaped glass and steel atrium, which consists of glass walls intersecting with the white keel-shaped steel roof supported by a full-height column at each end (Fig.1).

The keel roof achieves a long span using a tied arch built up of steel pipes and cables (Fig. 2), while giving the appearance of the bottom of a boat keel suspended in air. As the tied arch structure is self-reacting, no horizontal thrust nor bending moment is imposed on the end columns.

Furthermore, vertical cables in the glass side walls pull down on the keel roof. These cables are pre-tensioned to improve stability against wind, which can produce compression in the end columns in excess of the roof's self-weight. Pre-tension was introduced by pulling the cables down using a jack and then fixing the lower connections.

Lateral force resistant system adds to the architectural flair

The columns alone would be insufficient during a major earthquake, and so the columns are connected at three floors to increase the lateral stiffness and reduce the roof response. Furthermore, the glass walls attract large wind forces and so vertical cable trusses were provided to withstand these horizontal forces. The triangular bridges connecting the two sides of the hall function as diaphragms, transferring the horizontal wind forces to the sub-structure braced frame. This articulated structural system is used to accentuate the architecture.

1 / Interior view: The slope of the glass building and the diagonal corridors provide resistance to the large wind pressure acting on the wall surface.

2 / Cables extend onto the glass walls on both sides to stabilize the roof

3-5-1 Marunouchi, Chiyoda-ku, Tokyo
Architectural Design: Rafael Viñoly Architects Office
Structural design: Structural design group (SDG)
Construction: Obayashi Corporation and Kajima Corporation
Completion: 1996
Structure type: Steel structure

Mitsubishi Ichigokan Museum

Meiji architecture born in Heisei dynasty

Pioneer of Marunouchi business district

At the northwest corner of the intersection of Babasaki-dori and Daimyo-koji, there is a Victorian architecture surrounded by skyscrapers. The original one, completed in 1894, was built as a herald building of the modern business district at that time in Marunouchi, and was a rental office that tenanted banks etc. Architectural designer was Josiah Conder (1852–1920). The area around Babasaki-dori, where English-style office buildings were built one after another around this building, was later called "Iccho London (London corner)". The building was a brick structure constructed on 5,000 pine stakes as piles, with European timber roof trusses, and openings in the brick walls were reinforced by iron bands. Although it was recognized as a historically important building, it was demolished with little respect in 1968 in the tide of high growth period. Forty years later, in 2009, the building was rebuilt with brickwork as part of redevelopment in Marunouchi area. The restored building employs seismic isolation system with 33 laminated rubber bearings on the concrete slab foundation. The superstructure was restored as faithfully as possible to the original from the construction method to the detailed decoration. 2.3 million bricks were procured from China, where the manufacturing method is close to the Japanese one in the Meiji period, and were carefully piled up. Brick reinforcement by iron bands and roof trusses including metal connections were faithfully reproduced. The restaurant is well designed, restoring the bank office, and is worth seeing.

Pine stakes which supported buildings in Marunouchi

Pine stakes are extremely durable in water. Because Marunouchi area is on the stratum of deep alluvium and have extremely poor ground many pine stakes were used for the foundation. A long pine stake that supported the old Marunouchi Building is embedded and on display in the entrance hall floor along Gyoko-dori in the current Marunouchi Building.

1–2 / Queen Anne style appearance
3–4 / Pine stake displayed in the current Marunouchi Building

2-6-2 Marunouchi, Chiyoda-ku, Tokyo
Architectural design & Structural design: Mitsubishi Jisho Sekkei
Construction: Takenaka Corporation
Completion of the restored building: 2009
Structure type: Brick masonry structure, seismic isolation structure

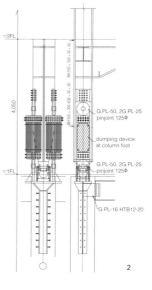

1 / Façade at night
2 / Detail of Stepping column system

Maison Hermès
Glowing modern five-storied pagoda

Stepping columns that allow vertical movement of the building

This building is for the Asia headquarters of Hermes. The façade, finished with specially designed glass blocks, illuminate the city of Ginza at night. The designer Renzo Piano calls it a "magic lantern."

For the realization of the design image of the store, a clear distinction of different structural roles was set up between the core part, which bears the seismic force, and the pin columns in the store, which support only building's self-weight. The beams on the store side have enough strength to hold the frames of the glass blocks hung at their tips, and the deformation of the tips is controlled by the pin columns. For this reason, the stiffness of the beam can be reduced, and the unfavorable extra stress to the pin columns is minimized, when the beam works as an outrigger of the building.

Stepping column system

An innovative structural system was adopted in this building. That is the "stepping column system", specially developed for a building with a tower-like proportion, a structural system that absorbs seismic energy by lifting up the column bases vertically. The most important feature of this system is autonomy. The columns are lifted off when the seismic load reaches a certain level. Then the natural period of the building changes. The natural period and damping increase, thereby reducing the seismic force. This was the world's first application of this system to a building structure.

Cutting-edge autonomous damping structure

The unique point of this system is that the damping system is not controlled by any sensors or computers, but the building responds to the external force and gains damping effect by itself, (according to the result of study, the base shear coefficient was reduced by about 40%).

It is said that the secret of the survival of five-story pagodas in Japan in many major earthquakes is the reduction of seismic energy due to the lifting of the column foot and the energy absorption due to sinking in member joints. The engineers of this building applied these ideas to the building with modern structural technology and well answered to the architectural design requirement.

5-4-1 Ginza, Chuo-ku, Tokyo
Architectural Design: Renzo Piano Building Workshop, Rena Dumas Architecture Intérieure, Takenaka Corporation
Structural design: Arup
Construction: Takenaka Corporation   Completion: 2001
Structure type: Steel structure

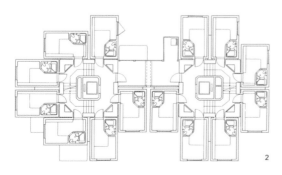

1 / Exterior view of the tower

2 / Plan view

Nakagin Capsule Tower Building

A housing complex embodying Metabolism

A Shape of Metabolism

The Nakagin Capsule Tower is a monumental building of Metabolism, a Japanese architectural and urban design movement in 1960–70's. Core elements, such as elevators and stairs, necessary for human mobility, water supply and drainage piping, and electrical wiring are rather permanent and fixed at the shaft structure. On the other hand, housings should be replaceable along with change of lifestyles. Therefore, the designers adopted the idea of Metabolism to buildings, integrating the functions of the house into a capsule unit, and made it possible to replace them as a unit when it is necessary. In the capsule unit, a bed, storage, a desk, a unit-bath (a prefabricated small one room unit with a bath, toilet and washbasin) and a sink are installed. It also features a signature 1300 mm diameter round window. This architecture gave a shape to the idea of the movement in an easy-to-understand manner. Due to the decrepitude, demolition of the building has been discussed. However, there are many voices calling for preservation.

Installation of core shafts and capsules

There are two core shafts of SRC structure and capsules are attached to a shaft in a pair, arranging two units in a vertical line. Each core shaft is a tower of a 5 m square plan having an elevator in the center and stairs around it. Each tower has a dense rigid frame structure with steel columns at the corners and at the center of the side. Two towers are structurally connected by beams on the second floor to resist tilting moment during earthquakes.

The capsule is of a minimum size with 2.5 m width, 4 m depth and 2.2 m ceiling height. This size was ruled by the size of trailer container used to transport the capsule. The structure of the capsule is a lightweight steel all-welded truss box. A total of 8 patterns were prepared, and the exterior of the building is characterized by combination of these capsules arranged vertically and horizontally.

* The Nakagin Capsule Tower Building is scheduled to be dismantled after March 2022.

8-16-10 Ginza, Chuo-ku, Tokyo
Architectural Design: Kisho Kurokawa architects & associates
Structural design: Gengo Matsui + ORS office
Construction: Taisei Corporation
Completion: 1972
Structure type: SRC structure, partially S structure
Photo: Tomio Ohashi

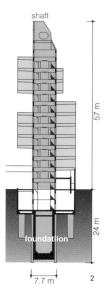

Shizuoka Press and Broadcasting Center in Tokyo

Tree-shaped architecture constructed on a huge foundation

Architecture consisting of a trunk, branches and leaves

When you head to Ginza from Shimbashi Station, you will see this uniquely shaped building standing at the corner of the intersection. It is an architectural work that perfectly matches the design and structural concept of "tree" by making the office part with light and supple steel construction and the shaft part with rigid steel reinforced concrete construction.

This design approach strongly reflects the influence of metabolism and is an attempt to reorganize the disorderly expanding city. It merges into a stream of Mr. Tange's design such as "A plan for Tokyo", "Yamanashi Press and Broadcasting Center" and "University of Oran". A huge shaft acts as a vertical artery for people and things, a cable for exchanging information, and a trunk line for energy supply and excretion. In a city scale, shafts are connected to each other by horizontally spreading branches and leaves and create a forest-like network. This building is designed using one shaft, which is the smallest element.

A huge root that supports tree

Since this building has the shape of a single tree with a height of 57 meters, a large overturning moment occurs at the foot when a horizontal force, such as seismic load, acts. To cope with this, caisson type piles, manually dug with special care, with a diameter of 7.7 meters and a depth of 24 meters underground are prepared as foundations. The large scale of the foundation gives an idea of the big challenge the structural designers had to face because of the large overturning moment. The lateral soil pressure on this huge foundation provides enough resistance to a large overturning moment during earthquakes.

It is our hope that not only the visible part on the ground, trunk, branches and leaves of the tree are recognized, but also the existence of the huge root that supports them under ground is also felt.

1 / Exterior view
2 / Section view

8-3-7 Ginza, Chuo-ku, Tokyo
Architectural design: Kenzo Tange + TANGE ASSOCIATES
Structural design: AOKI Shigeru laboratory
Construction: Taisei Corporation
Completion: 1967
Structure type: Steel reinforced concrete construction and Steel construction

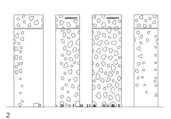

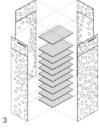

1 / Entire building
2 / Elevation
(From left to north, west,
south,east)
3 / Composition of steel plate
concrete building

MIKIMOTO Ginza 2
Free opening visualizing hybrid technology

Ingenious façade and space

MIKIMOTO Ginza 2 is a building that stands out in the Ginza Streets. Its distinctive façade has openings with a fluid pattern and a seamless finish. In this architecture, the surface and the structure are indivisible, which creates originality that is never overlooked in the surrounding environment even in Ginza where fashionable commercial buildings are lined up.

Structure of highly artistic design

This unique façade, which is also the structure encasing a 14 m × 17 m rectangular plan column-free space, supports the entire weight of the building. This façade is realized by a steel plate concrete structure, which is a composite structure of two steel plates tied together by studs keeping a gap which is filled with concrete. The filled concrete increases the rigidity of the building and stiffens the structure by preventing local buckling of steel plates, and all the load applied to the building is supported only by these steel plates. Filling the gap with concrete maximizes the strength of the steel plate, enabling it to support a height of 48 m with thin wall

thickness of just about 200 mm. In addition, for the fire-resistant design, the building is designed so that the concrete part can solely support the entire weight in case of fire. This eliminated the need to fireproof the steel part. As a result of these preparations, a seamless façade only covered by painting became possible. Considering the distortion during welding of the steel plates and the difference in area of the openings, the thickness of the steel plates were carefully chosen from 6 to 12 mm depending on the position on the façade.

Seamless façade

On-site welding was essential to construct an integrated steel plate concrete structural wall. The size of one steel plate panel is 2.4 m wide while the height is identical to the floor height (4.5 m or 5.0 m). They are welded together to form a 48 m high exterior wall, which surrounds floors of 14 m × 17 m in plan. It is said that the total length required to weld together the steel plate panels during the construction was over 6800 m. The welded part was ground to finish the surface smoothly.

2-4-12 Ginza, Chuo-ku, Tokyo
Architectural Design: Toyo Ito & Associate, Architects, Taisei Corporation
Structural design: Mutsuro Sasaki and Partners, Taisei Corporation
Construction: Taisei Corporation
Completion: 2005
Structure type: Steel plate concrete structure, some wall type reinforced concrete construction

Chapter 4

Harajuku & Aoyama & Roppongi

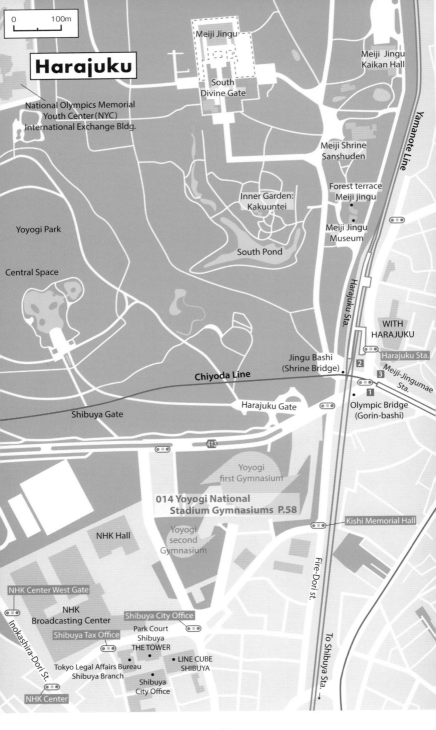

Harajuku

Meiji Jingu

Meiji Jingu Kaikan Hall

South Divine Gate

National Olympics Memorial Youth Center (NYC) International Exchange Bldg.

Meiji Shrine Sanshuden

Inner Garden: Kakuuntei

Forest terrace Meiji jingu

Yoyogi Park

Meiji Jingu Museum

Central Space

South Pond

Yamanote Line

WITH HARAJUKU

Harajuku Sta.

Jingu Bashi (Shrine Bridge)

2 Harajuku Sta.

Chiyoda Line

3 Meiji-Jingumae Sta.

1

Shibuya Gate

Harajuku Gate

Olympic Bridge (Gorin-bashi)

413

Yoyogi first Gymnasium

014 Yoyogi National Stadium Gymnasiums P.58

NHK Hall

Yoyogi second Gymnasium

Kishi Memorial Hall

Fire-Dori st.

NHK Center West Gate

NHK Broadcasting Center

Shibuya City Office

Shibuya Tax Office

Park Court Shibuya THE TOWER

Inokashira-Dori St.

Tokyo Legal Affairs Bureau Shibuya Branch

LINE CUBE SHIBUYA

To Shibuya Sta.

Shibuya City Office

NHK Center

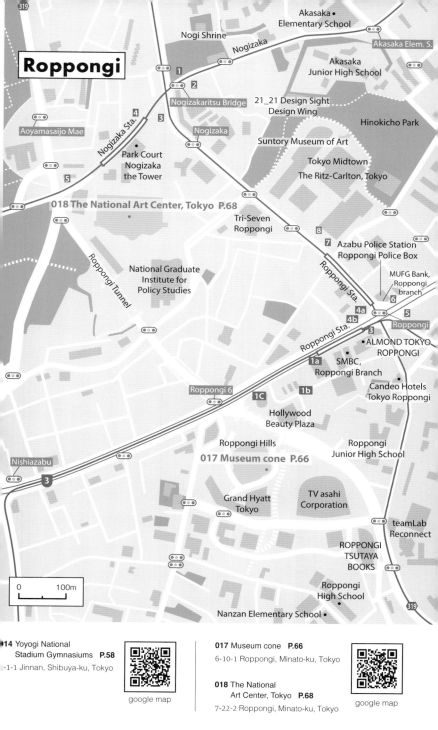

Roppongi

Nogi Shrine
Nogizaka
Akasaka • Elementary School
Akasaka Elem. S.

Akasaka Junior High School

1
2
Nogizakaritsu Bridge
21_21 Design Sight
Design Wing

Hinokicho Park

4
3
Aoyamasaijo Mae
Nogizaka
Nogizaka Sta.
Suntory Museum of Art

Park Court Nogizaka the Tower

5
Tokyo Midtown
The Ritz-Carlton, Tokyo

018 The National Art Center, Tokyo **P.68**

Tri-Seven Roppongi

Roppongi Tunnel
National Graduate Institute for Policy Studies

8
7
Azabu Police Station
Roppongi Police Box

Roppongi Sta.
MUFG Bank, Roppongi branch
6

4a
4b
5
3
Roppongi Sta.
Roppongi

• ALMOND TOKYO ROPPONGI

1a
SMBC, Roppongi Branch

Roppongi 6
1C
1b

• Candeo Hotels Tokyo Roppongi

Hollywood Beauty Plaza

Roppongi Hills
017 Museum cone **P.66**
Roppongi Junior High School

Nishiazabu
3
Grand Hyatt Tokyo
TV asahi Corporation

teamLab Reconnect

ROPPONGI TSUTAYA BOOKS

Roppongi High School

Nanzan Elementary School •

| 0 | 100m |

Omotesando, Aoyama

To Yoyogi Sta.

To Kita-sando Sta.

Harajuku Gaien
Junior High School

Harajukugaienchu W.

Jingumae 1

Togo Shrine

Harajuku
Police Station

Togo
Kinenkan

Takeshita St.

Harajuku Sta.

WITH
HARAJUKU

Togo Jinja Shrine

Harajuku Sta.

Takeshita

Fukutoshin Line

2

3

To Yoyogi Park

Meiji-jingumae Sta.

Laforet
Harajuku

1

Jingumae

5

6

4

Tokyu Plaza
Omotesando
Harajuku

Jingumae
Elementary School

Meiji-jingumae
Sta.

7

413

MUFG
Bank
ATM

GYRE

DIOR
Omotesando

Omotesando
Hills

Yamanote Line

305

Meiji-dori
Ave.

Louis Vuitton
Omotesando

Fukutoshin Line

To Shibuya Sta.

To Shibuya Sta.

United Nations
University

021 House of the Tower P.73

Shibuya-ku, Tokyo

google map

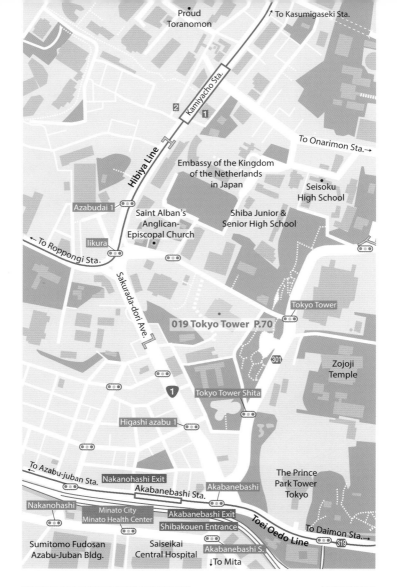

Proud
Toranomon

To Kasumigaseki Sta.

Kamiyacho Sta.

2 | 1 |

Hibiya Line

To Onarimon Sta.→

Embassy of the Kingdom
of the Netherlands
in Japan

Seisoku
High School

Azabudai 1

Saint Alban's
Anglican-
Episcopal Church

Shiba Junior &
Senior High School

← To Roppongi Sta.

Iikura

Sakurada-dori Ave.

Tokyo Tower

019 Tokyo Tower P.70

301

Zojoji
Temple

1

Tokyo Tower Shita

Higashi azabu 1

To Azabu-juban Sta.

Nakanohashi Exit

Akabanebashi Sta.

Akabanebashi

The Prince
Park Tower
Tokyo

Nakanohashi

Minato City
Minato Health Center

Akabanebashi Exit

Shibakouen Entrance

Toei Oedo Line

To Daimon Sta.→

319

Sumitomo Fudosan
Azabu-Juban Bldg.

Saiseikai
Central Hospital

Akabanebashi S.

↓To Mita

Akabanebashi, Kamiyacho

google map

019 Tokyo Tower **P.70**

4-2-8 Shibakoen, Minato-ku, Tokyo

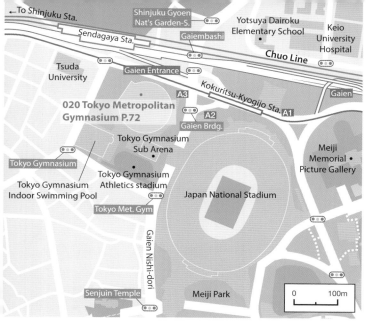

Sendagaya

020 Tokyo Metropolitan Gymnasium   **P.72**

1-17-1 Sendagaya, Shibuya-ku, Tokyo

google map

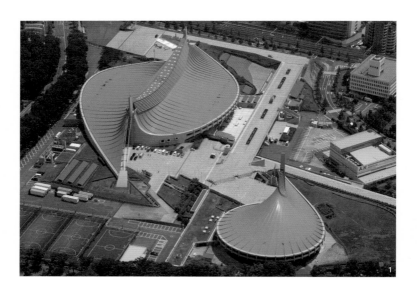

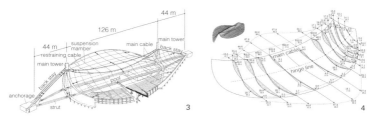

1 / Bird's eye view: top left, first gymnasium. bottom right, second gymnasium.

2 / Appearance of first gymnasium

3 / Diagram of the structural system of first gymnasium. Pay attention to the overall equilibrium system including the underground struts.

4 / The tension and bending moment diagram acting on the hanging members. The unit of force is ton (t, about 10 kN) in the notation at that time.

Yoyogi National Stadium Gymnasiums
Ever-stimulating design

The first gymnasium

Yoyogi National Stadium was built as an athletic facility for swimming (first gymnasium) and basketball (second gymnasium) on the occasion of the 1964 Tokyo Olympics. In spite of an extremely short work period, the design and construction were carried out with full enthusiasm to realize a unique large-span suspended roof structure in the world, for the first Olympic games in Japan. Even now, half a century after its completion, the design of this stadium doesn't grow old.

The first gymnasium is a suspended roof structure with a circular plan of about 120 m diameter having extra spans for the entrances on both sides. The pair of main cables forming the central span adopts a structural principle similar to a suspension bridge but differs from it in many aspects. For example, the plane of the backstay is not parallel to the axis of the building and the main cables are wide open in the center to create the space of skylights and artificial lighting (Figure 3). The roof surface is formed from many semi-rigid hanging members (tension members with flexural rigidity) that run from the main cable to the stadium stand. In addition, to achieve uniform stiffness in the roof, a series of restraining cables is arranged running through the hanging members, and by tensioning these cables the whole roof system is prestressed. Figure 4 shows stress distribution of the semi-rigid suspension members (under vertical load and prestress). At that time, the concept of a semi-rigid suspended roof structure had not yet been developed anywhere int the world. Then the stress and deformation of the roof structure were calculated starting from establishing a fundamental formula, linearizing it, and solving it with a hand-operated mechanical calculator. In recent years, the same structure was recalculated by computers and it was confirmed that the results at that time were sufficiently accurate (Figure 4).

The main cables forming the central span show significant deformation, about 2 meters at center of the span, especially during construction. In order to follow the complex relative displacement of the joint, a cast steel joint, resembling the ring of Saturn, that can rotate freely in any direction and is used to connect the hanging member and the main cable. Because an identical shape of the joint can accommodate any position it is highly reasonable to produce them by casting.

World's first vibration control structure

Since the roof structure of Yoyogi Stadium is relatively lightweight, it was important to consider the safety against wind load. Regarding the static effect of the wind, safety was confirmed by verification based on wind tunnel experi-

5 / A "Ring of Saturn" joint can be seen up close near the entrance. The joints in the arena can also be observed if you bring in a telescope.

6 / The oil dampers (2 layers × 3 units) installed near the capital are painted red and can be recognized from the outside.

7 / Interior view of first gymnasium.

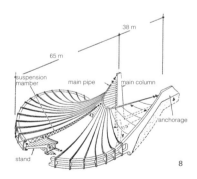

8 / Diagram of the structural system of second gymnasium. The main pipe running from the capital of the main column to the anchor block forms the core of the structure.

9 / Sculpturally impressive form integrated by main columns, main pipes, and struts.

ment, but regarding the dynamic response, considering that the building was likely to be used as an emergency control center in the event of a disaster, vibration control system was designed to reduce unforeseen dynamic deformations of the main cable. Vibration is controlled by absorbing energy with six oil dampers installed near the capital on each side (Figure 6).

The second gymnasium

The second gymnasium has a circular plan with a diameter of 65 meters. The structural principle of this architecture is the same as that of the first gymnasium, but the central structure is formed by a main pipe that runs spirally from the top of the single main column toward the anchorage (Figure 8). The spatial curve created by this main pipe is close to the curve defined by one of the three-dimensional funicular polygon drawn with the force at the end of the hanging steel frame attached to it, but due to architectural requirements, it deviates from this curve of equilibrium to some extent. In order to stably handle this deviation and change of a hanging member tension due to load fluctuation, a group of struts, which form one three-dimensional truss by integrating these with the main pipe, are provided between the main pipe and the column and function as supports for the top light sash.

Unlike the main cable of the first gymnasium, the main pipe of the second gymnasium does not have backstay. For this reason, a large bending moment is always generated in the main column and the tie beam. To cope with this large bending and to prevent rigidity reduction by clacks, prestress is applied to both by the post-tensioning. The hanging members of the roof are designed as steel trusses with enough height connected each other expecting shell effect as a whole. There are no restraining cables in this roof. That is a different point from the first gymnasium.

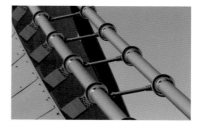

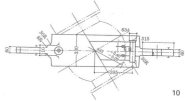

10

10 / The cast steel joint, resembling the ring of Saturn.

2-1-1 Jinnan, Shibuya-ku, Tokyo
Architectural design: TANGE ASSOCIATES
Structural design: TSUBOI Yoshikatsu laboratory
Construction: Shimizu Corporation
Structure type: Steel-suspended roof structure

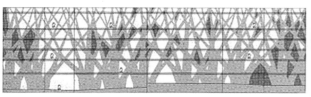

TOD'S Omotesando

Graphic inspired dendritic RC structure

RC silhouette of zelkova trees

A distinctive building can be found on the left when walking from the Tokyu Metro Omotesando Station towards the Meiji Jingu Shrine, featuring a façade that mimics the silhouette of zelkova trees (Fig. 1). Exposed reinforced concrete (RC) "branches" spread organically upward from the "trunk", while sashless double-glazed glass panels fill the gaps. While "glass box" commercial buildings with a steel frame and glass curtain walls are common, what makes this building unique is the eye-catching dendritic RC structure.

Toyo Ito Architects previously realized similar aesthetics in temporary structures such as the "Brugge Pavilion (2002)", but this was their first full-scale permanent building in this graphic architectural style. A paper cutout model used in the design phase is shown in Fig. 2.

The organic shape of the tree, where the branches gradually thin from the base to the top, follows the same structural rationality as engineered structures with column sizes that increase with accumulating forces along the height from the top to bottom. The larger openings at the upper floors are taken advantage of by placing the offices and party rooms on these floors.

Dendritic branches act as seismic braces

There are no interior columns nor beams, and the dendrite perimeter columns are only 300 mm, thinner than typical RC structures. Nevertheless, the diagonal dendritic columns provide significant lateral stiffness and strength, acting similar to a braced frame in a conventional steel or timber structure. The building is also seismically isolated, with the seismic isolation plane located in the basement. The construction required close collaboration between the structural design team and the contractor to resolve challenges such as arranging the reinforcing bars intersecting at different angles and the fabrication and installation of about 270 different glass pane sizes.

1 / Appearance mimicking a row of zelkova trees
2 / Transformation of the horizontal zelkova pattern into the L-shaped outer wall.

5-1-5 Jingumae, Shibuya-ku, Tokyo
Architectural Design: Toyo Ito & Associates, Architects
Structural design: Oak structural design
Construction: Takenaka Corporation
Completion: 2004
Structure type: RC structure (Penthouse: Steel structure)

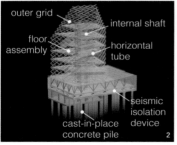

outer grid

internal shaft

floor assembly

horizontal tube

seismic isolation device

cast-in-place concrete pile

1 / The façade surrounded by diagonal grids is impressive
2 / Structural diagram   3 / State during construction

Prada Aoyama

Glass jewelry box made possible by seismic isolation

Design of latticed perimeter members

Prada Aoyama was the first project in Japan by the Swiss architect Herzog & de Meuron. It has a jewel-like appearance with the outer shape defined by a chiseled diagonal pattern and daylighting controlled by the opacity of diamond glass panels (Fig. 1). The structure has few columns, instead featuring a perimeter diagonal lattice, the pitch and angle of which were determined from the angled design surface.

The superstructure has a steel frame, with the perimeter diagrid and columns around the stairs as the sole vertical load bearing members. Although the outer dimensions of the diagrid members are all equal, the stress applied to each is different and so seven section sizes were used, each with a different plate thickness, the thickest up to 60 mm.

A pure diagonal grid has a disadvantage in transmitting vertical loads, in that it tends to spread out like a pantograph (free to rotate at the joints). To prevent this, horizontal connecting beams are placed along outer edges of each floor and connected to the diagrid, suppressing the spreading effect and limiting the vertical dead load displacement at the top to 3 cm. A jack was also used during construction to lift each grid by up to 3 mm to ensure the correct position. However, some of the lattice members near to the stairwell resist smaller axial forces, yet are mixed with highly loaded members, complicating the vertical position corrections.

Introduction of seismic isolation

The outer dimensions of the lattice members were limited to just 150 × 250 mm, which could only be achieved by reducing the inertial forces during major earthquakes. The seismic forces in the upper part of the building were controlled by introducing seismic isolation bearings under the first basement floor. This made it possible to realize a light European design in earthquake-prone Japan. However, the silhouette of the lattice members is slightly larger when viewed from the inside, as the steel members are encased in 50 mm thick fireproof coating. A fitting room with a diamond-shaped cross section penetrates the glass box, and was constructed with a monocoque structure made of steel plates, similar to a ship bulkhead.

In the event of a major earthquake, the moss-covered expansion joint panels encircling the isolated structure at ground level will pop up, permitting the building to move freely.

5-2-6 Minami Aoyama, Minato-ku, Tokyo
Architectural design: Herzog & de Meuron Architecten, Takenaka Corporation
Structural design: Takenaka Corporation
Construction: Takenaka Corporation   Completion: 2003
Structure type: S structure, RC structure

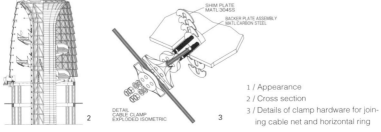

SHIM PLATE
MATL:304SS

BACKER PLATE ASSEMBLY
MATL:CARBON STEEL

DETAIL
CABLE CLAMP
EXPLODED ISOMETRIC

1 / Appearance

2 / Cross section

3 / Details of clamp hardware for join-
ing cable net and horizontal ring

Museum cone
Transparent glass architecture with horizontal rings

Tapered elliptical glass cone

An elliptical transparent glass body stands at the corner of Roppongi Hills marking the entrance to the Mori Art Museum. The cone-like structure overlooks the Mori Garden and offers excellent views of the upper part of Roppongi Hills.

The space is defined by a central elevator core encircled by a spiral staircase and outer glass curtain wall. White dots of ceramic paint are baked into the glass to create completely different looks in daylight and after dark.

Structural system with funnel, horizontal ring plate and cable net

All of the spatial components act as structural members. The glass curtain wall is directly supported by 12 tiers of horizontal steel ring plates with gradually changing diameters that follow the elliptical shape. Each horizontal ring plate is clamped to a two-directional cable net, which is stretched in spirals from the top of the central elevator core to the base. The funnel-shaped elevator core is a braced steel frame with a diameter that gradually expands up the height. By pre-tensioning the cable net, which places the ring beams and ele-vator core in compression, the structure remains stable against all loading types.

The spiral staircase is supported by cantilever plates extending from the elevator core, and is offset from the curtain wall.

Details that support the transparent body

The core, cable, ring beam, and glass facet details were carefully designed to achieve a stunning transparency. The clamped connections between the cable net and the horizontal ring beams are particularly notable. Due to the tapered elliptical shape, this connection had to be designed to easily accommodate different connecting angles.

The ingenious structure results in the metal joints and cables being barely noticeable and places the visual emphasis on the horizontal ring plates, which appear to be white rings floating in the air.

6-10-1 Roppongi, Minato-ku, Tokyo
Architectural design: Mori Building, Gluckman Mayner
Structural design: Yoshinori Nito + Yumi Nawa, Dewhurst Macfarlane and Partners
Construction: Obayashi / Kashima Joint Venture
Completion: 2003
Structure type: steel structure

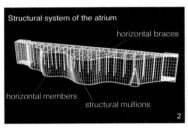

Structural system of the atrium

horizontal braces

horizontal members

structural mullions

1 / Curved glass façade
2 / Structural perspective
3 / Interior view of the glass atrium
4 / Exhibition room
5 / Aerial view

The National Art Center, Tokyo
Mullion integrated glass curtain walls

Curved mullions as columns

Tokyo's National Art Center, with its un-dulating curved glass façade, is the largest museum in Japan. It is located adjacent to the Nogizaka Station on the Chiyoda Line. It does not have own col-lection, but rather hosts public and spe-cial exhibitions. A curved glass atrium is attached to a 130 by 60 by 23 m box, housing the main exhibit space. The atrium is spacious as there are no free-standing interior columns. Even the lob-by appears open due to the ample light streaming through the glass curtain wall. Large-area curtain walls are typi-cally subjected to large wind pressures in the out-of-plane direction, and so mullions (thin vertical members) are provided to support the glass façade.

The mullions were made slightly thicker and were connected to horizon-tal members to prevent buckling, en-abling them to function as columns supporting the roof. At first glance, the columns appear to be bent or falling outward, puzzling onlookers as to how they could support the roof. Having been designed in the shape of a curved surface, the mullions and horizontal members (transoms) were efficiently utilized to realize this delicate mullion integrated glass curtain wall.

Invisible structure

Although the structural frame is hidden, various techniques were applied to re-alize this "invisible" structure. The large exhibition room features staggered cores spaced at 34.2 m and spanned using 2.25 m deep trusses. The seismic response is controlled using seismic base isolation, while tuned mass damp-ers are installed on the long span beams to reduce the vertical response. This seismic response control system enabled the architects and designers to realize the large exhibition space.

Memory of history

The visitor can find a small pavilion in front of the entrance. This is the partial remains of the building of the institute of Industrial Science at the University of Tokyo, originally built as a Japanese army station. It used to be a huge build-ing occupying the whole site of this art center. A model of this historic building is displayed at the entrance area of the complex.

7-22-2 Roppongi, Minato-ku, Tokyo
Architectural design: Kisho Kurokawa Architects and Urban Design Office, Nihon Sekkei Community
Structural design: Nihon Sekkei
Construction: Joint Venture by Kashima, Taisei, Matsumura JV, Shimizu, Obayashi and Mitsui
Completion: 2006
Structure type: Steel reinforced concrete structure (SRC)

1–2 / Tokyo Tower at the time of construction and now
3 / Lifting of SG Tower (Photo courtesy: Takenaka Corporation)
4 / The guide derrick relocated on the truss (Photo courtesy: Takenaka Corporation)

Tokyo Tower

Symbol of Tokyo, ever progressing with structural technology in the successive eras

A tallest class free-standing steel tower

At the start of television broadcasting, during the post-war reconstruction period in Japan, every TV station in Tokyo was independently beginning to build their own transmission towers. Tokyo Tower was constructed as a comprehensive radio tower, covering the entire Kanto region, meeting and unifying these demands.

The height of 333 m was outstanding in the world at that time. The big project was a symbol of remarkable and progressive reconstruction of Japan.

Tower representing structural rationality

Economic performance, practicality, and safety were the top priorities in the design.

The estimation of wind load in the structural design was set high enough even compared to current standards.

Dr. Tachu Naito said, "As a result of pursuing lean and stable products with safety, we created beauty led by numbers, rather than artificial aesthetic".

In the comparison with the Eiffel Tower in Paris (324 m, completed in 1889), which used 7,300 t of steel for its frame and was constructed in 27 months, Tokyo Tower used 3,600 t steel and was completed in 18 months.

Member design and Foundation

Each member was meticulously designed using a slide rule and a Cremona graphic statics.

The main frame of the tower is a truss skeleton as an assemblage of members built with simple profiled members. The super gain (SG) tower at the top uses high-tensile round steel to reduce the wind load effect.

The reinforced concrete piles are connected diagonally to take the thrust force at the tower base.

Construction method

A "guide derrick crane" was set on the ground and used for the construction of four tower legs. When the tower reached 53 m high, it was raised and put on the tower truss and used for the next stage up to 120 m. After that, up to 250 m, a hanging type "erector" placed in the center was used to lift members, including SG tower.

4-2-8 Shibakoen, Minato-ku, Tokyo
Design: Nikken Sekkei Ltd.
Design guidance: Tachuu Naito
Construction: Takenaka Corporation
Completion: 1958
Structure type: Steel construction

TOKYO METROPOLITAN GYMNASIUM

Tokyo Metropolitan Gymnasium
Load bearing keel arches

Two leaves covering a circular roof

The complex consists of the main arena, a smaller arena, and pool, with the main arena a particularly fine example of collaborative architectural and structural design.

The arena is surrounded by a plaza for people to roam around and a low roofline provided so that it does not dominate the surroundings. This gives the appearance of a slender long-span structure fit in a narrow space between the roof and ceiling. Furthermore, the basement was dug down as low as possible to the given water-table height, so that the building stays mostly underground to bringing the roof closer into view at ground level. When viewed from above, two large leaves may be seen covering the circular roof.

Low-rise arch

The roof structure consists of two lower arches that trace the main veins of the leaves, with two upper arches extending up to the center of the roof. Truss beams branch out from arches to the roof perimeter.

Each of the lower arches resist 50% of the load through bending action, while the remainder via arch action. The circular center arches are angled, such that they arch in both the vertical and horizontal directions, with the thrust resisted at each end by the lower arches. The arches and truss beams are visible from inside of the arena, allowing visitors to easily visualize the flow of forces.

1-17-1 Sendagaya, Shibuya-ku, Tokyo
Architectural design: Maki General Planning Office / Structural design: Toshihiko Kimura Architects
Construction: Joint Venture by Shimizu Construction, Tokyu Construction, Konoike Construction, Dai Nippon Construction and Ogawa Construction
Completion: 1990   Structure type: Steel reinforced concrete structure (SRC)

1F carport   2F living·dining   3F bath room   4F bed room   5F kids room   0 1 3m

House of the Tower
A masterpiece of small urban housing

The house, standing on a tiny triangular site of 20 m², is the result of the architect's attempt to build his own home in a large city. He had to reserve sufficient space for a living while only 10 m² was available for each level. With such extreme physical constraints and a limited budget, no structural method other than load-bearing reinforced concrete walls made sense. Since a building code for constructing walls at non-orthogonal angles didn't exist, the project was developed through numerous discussions with structural engineers and a building official.

Partitions and doors between the rooms, including the restroom and bathroom, are eliminated to create a spatial flow inside the small, slender building. Furthermore, the architect elaborated on the height differences and placement of openings in the walls and floor slabs in pursuit of a small yet open space where each family member can sense one another through details such as open ceilings and gaps between stair treads. The house, with a rich living space hidden inside the crude concrete walls, is now known as a masterpiece of small urban housing.

Shibuya-ku, Tokyo
Architectural design: Takamitsu Azuma
Construction: Nagano Construction Co.
Completion: 1966
Structure type: Reinforced Concrete Structure

Tokyo Metropolitan
Government Building

Shinjuku Mitsui Building

Shinjuku
Sumitomo Building

Keio Plaza
Hotel

Chapter 5

High-rise buildings & Seismic retrofit

High-rise buildings in Shinjuku

Shinjuku i-LAND Tower

NTT Docomo Yoyogi Building

Shinjuku Center Building

Shinjuku Nomura Building

Mode Gakuen Cocoon Tower

Sompo Japan Building

Main skyscrapers in western areas of Shinjuku station

Tokyo Metropolitan Government Building (243 m, 1991)
Shinjuku Mitsui Building (225 m, 1974)
Shinjuku Center Building (223 m, 1979)
Shinjuku Sumitomo Building (210 m, 1974)
Shinjuku Nomura Building (210 m, 1978)

Mode Gakuen Cocoon Tower (192 m, 2008)
Sompo Japan Building (200 m, 1976)
Shinjuku i-LAND Tower (189 m, 1995)
Keio Plaza Hotel (179 m, 1971)
NTT Docomo Yoyogi Building (240 m, 2000)

Shinjuku, Yoyogi

Marunouchi Line

Nishishinjuku Junior High School

Naruko Tenjin Shrine

Nishishinjuku sta.

Tokyo Medical Univ. Hosp.

1

2

Shinjuku Police St

The Parkhouse Nishi-Shinjuku Tower 60

Tokyo Medical University Hospital

Shinjuku i-LAND Tower

Shinjuku Police Station

E7

C13

SHINJUKU NOMURA BUILD

Sumitomo Fudosan Shinjuku Central Park Building

Hilton Tokyo

Tokyo Metropolitan Government-N.

Kita Dori

Sompo Japa Nipponko Insurance In

Shinjuku Chuo Park-N.

E4

E3

Tokyo Metropolitan Assembly-N.

Shinjuku Center Build

Kumanojinja Shrine

Odakyū Dai-ichi Seimei Building

Shinjuku Sumitomo Building

Shinjuku Mitsui Building

Honan-dori Ave.

Hyatt Regency Tokyo

A6

Chuo-dori

A5

A7

E2

Tochomae Sta.

A2

Kogakukan University Shinjuku Cam

Marunouchi Line

E1

Keio Plaza Hotel

A3

Shinjuku Chuo Park

A4

Tokyo Metropolitan Government Building No.1

022 Tokyo Metropolitan Government Building P.8

Shinjuku Chuo Park

Fureai-dori Ave.

Shinjuku Chuo Park-S.

Shinjuku Monolith Building

Shinjuku Chuo Park-W.

Tokyo Metropolitan Government Building No.2

Shinjuku NS Building

KDDI Building

Tokyo Metropolitan Assembly-S.

Tokyo Metropolitan Government-S.

Minami Dori

Nishishinjuku

Nishishinjuku Elementary School

Shinjuku

Shinjuku Washington Hotel

20

Nishishinjuku

Tsunohazu Civic Center

Koshu-Kaido Ave.

Keio Shinsen Line

Shinjuku Park Tower

Bunka Gakuen University

Nishishinjuku 3

New National Theatre, Tokyo

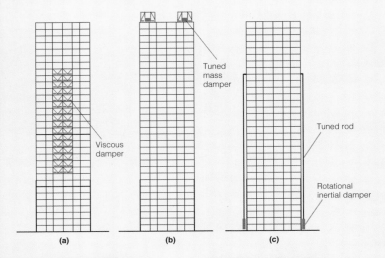

Types of seismic retrofit for high-rise buildings in Shinjuku

Tuned
mass
damper

Viscous
damper

Tuned rod

Rotational
inertial damper

(a)　　　　　　　(b)　　　　　　　(c)

The first high-rise blocks constructed in 1970's

In the western areas of Shinjuku station, you can find high-rise blocks occupied with around 20 high-rise buildings of 200 m to 300 m height which is rarely observed in a Japanese city. There used to be a large purification plant in this area, and the first 200 m class high-rise was initially constructed in the 1970's. Not only large free spaces could be obtained in this area, but with the Tokyo gravel layer placed at shallow underground, it was suitable to build skyscrapers. The first generation, Keio plaza hotel, Shinjuku Mitsui building, Shinjuku Sumitomo building, Shinjuku center building, Shinjuku Nomura building, Sonpo Japan building were constructed in 1970's, and followed by the second generation as Tokyo Metropolitan Government building, NTT Docomo building, and Mode Gakuen Cocoon Tower in 1990's to 2000's.

Seismic retrofit against long-duration shake

In 2011 Great East-Japan Earthquake, the damages of these high-rise buildings were negligible, however, seismic tremors with long natural period from far away exaggerated the shake of these skyscrapers and it continued for more than 10 minutes, causing seasickness in the occupants. For preventing such effects in the future earthquakes, seismic retrofit were carried out in all skyscrapers in 2010's. The retrofit method is mainly adding damping devises, and they can be categorized 1) adding viscous as damping braces in mid-stories (Shinjuku center building, Metropolitan Government building), 2) adding tuned mass dampers at the top (Shinjuku Mitsui Building) and 3) Tuned rod with rotational inertial damper working for the bending action of the building (Shinjuku Sumitomo building).

Type (a)
Shinjuku Center building

Type (b)
Shinjuku Mitsui Building

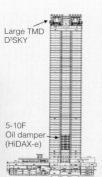

Large TMD
D³SKY

5-10F
Oil damper
(HiDAX-e)

Type (c)
Shinjuku Sumitomo building

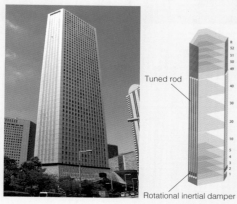
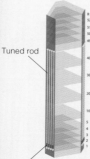

Tuned rod

Rotational inertial damper

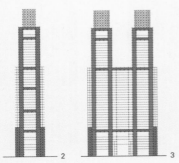

1 / Overall view
2 / Transversal section of the frame
3 / Longitudinal section of the frame

Tokyo Metropolitan Government Building
Mega-frame with mega-columns and mega-beams

Monumental skyscraper with Japanese traditional grid-like appearance

The Tokyo Metropolitan Government Building is located on the west side of Shinjuku. The stone exterior is reminiscent of an integrated circuit and gives the appearance of a traditional Japanese lattice. The complex actually consists of three buildings: the Parliament Building, 1st Government Building, and 2nd Government Building. The 1st Government Building splits into twin towers about halfway up, while the floorplate of the 2nd Government Building gradually changes.

The 1st Government Building is large, featuring 48 floors above ground, 243.4 m height, and a total floor area of 195,567 m², but it does not appear oppressive. This is probably because the exterior and form are designed in harmony with the surroundings, while giving a feeling of symbolism.

Regular structural plan by mega-frame

A highly earthquake-resistant structure was required, along with predominantly column-free office space and a flexible floorplan that could serve as an emergency response center in the event of a disaster. A simple and regular mega-frame (moment frame over multiple stories and bays) was adopted to realize this objective despite the complicated form and variation in the floor plan up the height of the building.

The mega-frame is assembled with four corner columns of 6.4 m square, which are connected with braces to form mega-columns. The floors hosting the machine rooms were then strengthened and braced to form mega-beams. By resisting the horizontal forces induced by earthquakes or typhoons through the mega-frame, it was possible to accommodate the complex setbacks and plan irregularities, which could be otherwise typically detrimental to the seismic performance. Furthermore, lateral deformation and overturning behavior, due to narrow entire profile with aspect ratio of over 7, in transversal direction, are effectively reduced.

2-8-1 Nishi-Shinjuku, Shinjuku-ku, Tokyo
Architectural Design: Kenzo Tange, Urban and Architectural Design Institute
Structural design: Mutoh Associates
Construction: Taisei Corporation, Shimizu Corporation, Takenaka Corporation, etc. JV
Completion: 1991
Structure type: S structure, some SRC / RC structure

Mode Gakuen Cocoon Tower
Structure that supports a huge cocoon

1 / Exterior of the building
2 / Inner core and Diana core frame

3D campus

The Mode Gakuen Cocoon Tower is a 204 m high-rise educational facility located in Nishi-Shinjuku with 50 aboveground stories. The silk-like strips entwined across the façade embody the "cocoon" design concept. Despite appearing to be a complex, irregular grid of braces, much of the façade linework is decorative. Triple-story student lounges provide community spaces to promote a sense of community and in-person communication, avoiding the siloed floors of typical high-rise buildings.

Inner core and diagrid frames

The superstructure consists of an inner core and three diagrid frames. The core is a moment frame with twelve 600 to 900 mm diameter CFT columns enveloping stairs and elevators. Three elliptical diagrid frames that consist primarily of 400 by 400 mm H-sections are arranged equidistantly along the perimeter and connected back to each other near the top (45th floor). The core plays a key role in controlling the seismic response as it features six oil dampers per floor.

*Only members and admission applicants are permitted inside.

1-7-3 Nishi-Shinjuku, Shinjuku-ku, Tokyo
Architectural Design:
Tange Urban Architects
Structural design: Arup Japan
Construction: Shimizu Corporation
Completion: 2008
Structure type: steel superstructure, concrete-filled steel tube columns, steel reinforced concrete substructure

NTT Docomo Yoyogi Building
New form of communication tower

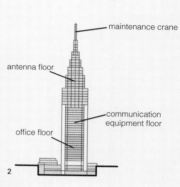

maintenance crane

antenna floor

communication
equipment floor

office floor

2

1 / Exterior of the building
2 / The office floor is up to the 26th floor, and above
  that is a communication tower structure.

Prominent site

The NTT Docomo Yoyogi Building is a skyscraper that both serves as an office and houses mobile phone communication equipment.

Give the prominent location, near the vast green spaces of Yoyogi Park, Shinjuku Gyoen National Garden and Meiji Jingu, there was concern that a 240 m skyscraper may significantly impact the cityscape. Consequently, the design adopted a Manhattan-style form that integrates the office building and communication tower into a seamless monolith, rather than the conventional approach of the antenna standing as a distinct element on top of the building.

True nature

Although the exterior gives the appearance of nearly 50 floors, in reality only the first 26th floors (about 100 m in height) are occupied, as the upper structure is a single story that houses the communication equipment. In essence, it is a hollow structure encasing antennas and cables.

Furthermore, the entire tapered upper volume hosts an antenna, while the red and white spire is actually a maintenance crane. If you look closely, the tip is divided into two parts that fold out when operating.

5-24-10 Sendagaya, Shibuya-ku, Tokyo
Construction: Kajima Corporation, Fujita, etc.
Architectural Design: NTT Facilities
Completion: 2000
Structural design: NTT Facilities
Structure type: Steel

Chapter 6

Bunkyo-ku

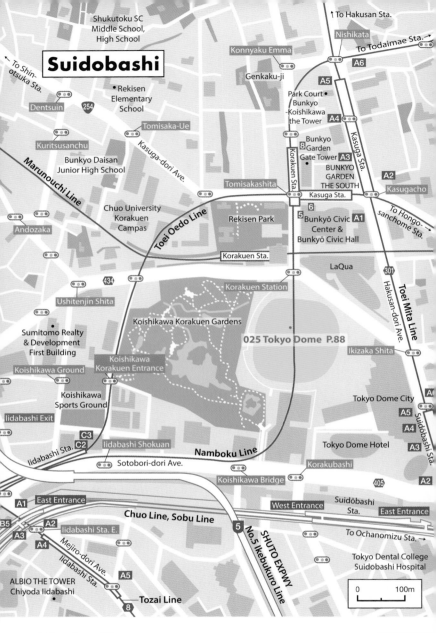

Suidobashi

Shukutoku SC Middle School, High School

→ To Hakusan Sta.

Nishikata

To Todaimae Sta. →

Konnyaku Emma

A6

Genkaku-ji

A5

Park Court Bunkyo -Koishikawa the Tower

A4

Kasuga Sta.

→ To Shin-otsuka Sta.

Rekisen Elementary School

Dentsuin

254

Tomisaka-Ue

Bunkyo Garden Gate Tower

A3

BUNKYO GARDEN THE SOUTH

Kuritsusanchu

Kasuga-dori Ave.

Bunkyo Daisan Junior High School

Marunouchi Line

Toei Oedo Line

Tomisakashita

A2

Kasugacho

Kasuga Sta.

To Hongo-sanchome Sta. →

Chuo University Korakuen Campas

Rekisen Park

Bunkyō Civic Center & Bunkyō Civic Hall

A1

Andozaka

434

Korakuen Sta.

LaQua

301

Ushitenjin Shita

Korakuen Station

Toei Mita Line

Hakusan-dori Ave.

Sumitomo Realty & Development First Building

Koishikawa Korakuen Gardens

025 Tokyo Dome P.88

Ikizaka Shita

Koishikawa Korakuen Entrance

Koishikawa Ground

Koishikawa Sports Ground

Tokyo Dome City

A5

Iidabashi Exit

A4

Suidōbashi Sta.

A3

C3

Tokyo Dome Hotel

C2

Iidabashi Shokuan

Namboku Line

A2

Iidabashi Sta.

Sotobori-dori Ave.

Korakubashi

405

Koishikawa Bridge

A1

East Entrance

Suidōbashi Sta.

West Entrance

East Entrance

B5

Chuo Line, Sobu Line

To Ochanomizu Sta. →

A2

Iidabashi Sta. E.

5

A3

SHUTO EXPWY No.5 Ikebukuro Line

A4

Mejiro-dori Ave.

Iidabashi Sta.

Tokyo Dental College Suidobashi Hospital

A5

ALBIO THE TOWER Chiyoda Iidabashi

Tozai Line

8

0   100m

025 Tokyo Dome **P.88**

1-3-61 Koraku, Bunkyo-ku, Tokyo

google map

Nihon Univ.
Buzan Junior & **1**
Senior High School

2

437

Gokoku-ji

3

Ochanomizu University
Junior High School

Gokokuji W. Gokokuji

4

Ochanomizu University
Senior High School

254

To
Kishibojimmae Sta.

Gokokuji S.

Ochanomizu
University
Elementary School

Special Needs
Education School
for the Visually Impaired,
University of Tsukuba

Ochanomizu University

SHUTO EXPWY No.5 Ikebukuro Line

Gokokuji Sta.

6 **5**

Kōdansha

Otsuka Police Station

Otowa
Junior High School

Otowa Dori

Senior High School
at Otsuka,
University of Tsukuba

To Kishibojimmae Sta.

Mejirodai 3

Tokyo College
of Music High School

435

Sekiguchidai
Park

026 St Mary's Cathedral P.90

5

Bunkyo Fukushi Center

Renkoji

Dokkyo Junior &
Senior High School

Yurakucho Line

Hotel
Chinzanso Tokyo

Mejiro Dori

8

Mejirosaka Shita

Sekiguchi Daimachi
Elementary School

Edogawa Park

5

Dainichizaka Shita

Hanamizubashi

To Waseda Sta.

8

Kanda River

1a

Shinmejiro-dori Ave.

Waseda Exit

Ikkyubashi Entrance

Tsurumakicho

Edogawabashi

1b **2**

Edogawa
bashi-dori

Edogawabashi Sta.

3

4

Gokokuji, Edogawabashi

0   100m

026 St Mary's Cathedral **P.90**

3-16-5 Sekiguchi, Bunkyo-ku, Tokyo

google map

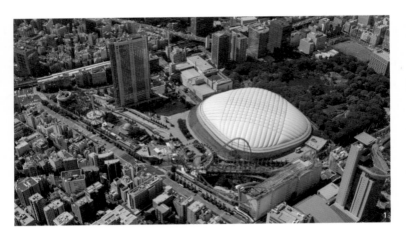

1 / Exterior view. The outer perimeter is a glass canopy with a three-dimensional truss

2 / Interior view   3 / Inflation in progress

Various types of pneumatic membrane structures

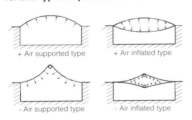

+ Air supported type

+ Air inflated type

- Air supported type

- Air inflated type

Blower that keeps blowing air into the internal space

Air-supported and air-inflated membranes are fundamental types of pneumatic roof structures. Air-supported type has a single layer of membrane and the whole interior space under the membrane is pressurized. The room requires special air-tight doors such as revolving doors for entry. Air-inflated type has two layers of membrane and space between them is pressurized. It is like an aircushion. Space under the roof does not require any pressure control. Either types can be pressurized positively or negatively. For positive type air inside takes compression stress while tension for negative type. Tokyo Dome is an air-supported type while the roofs for Tokyo international airport terminal II or Shin-toyosu Brillia running stadium are air-inflated cushions of ETFE foils.

Tokyo Dome

Large arena supported by air

Giant white melon bread

There is a huge white dome beside an amusement park, Tokyo Dome City. When you get closer to the dome, you will see that the tent-like roof membrane is inflated like a balloon. The material of the roof is a glass fiber textile coated with fluorine resin. This membrane material is strong and highly durable. The air inside the dome lifts the membrane roof, which is only 0.8 mm thick. The air inside plays the role of a pillar for the roof. In order to keep sufficient tension, the inflated membrane surface is divided into smaller sections and pulled down by a grid-like network of reinforcing cables. This is why there are many convex rectangular segments on the roof surface, which shape it like a melon bread. The air pressure difference between the inside and outside of the dome to lift the roof membrane is usually about 300 Pa, and in the case of snow or typhoons, it can be raised up to 900 Pa.

In addition, there are inner membranes suspended inside, and it is possible to melt snow by sending warm air between the inner and roof membranes. The entire roof structure is tilted by about the angle of 1/10 so that the dome roof does not interfere with sunlight to the adjacent botanical garden.

The first large-scale permanent air-supported dome in Japan

Air-supported structures have been developed in the United States since the 1950s, and then the low rise cable reinforced air-supported dome was developed for a large span structure exceeding 100 m. It debuted as the US Pavilion at the Osaka Expo in Japan in 1970. David Geiger, who invented the system, has since built numerous air-supported arenas in the US. This structure, which allows abundant daylight to its interior space through the membrane material, was in great demand as a covered sports facility for baseball and American football in US. 18 years after the Osaka Expo, the air-supported dome has returned to Japan as Tokyo Dome, first covered baseball stadium in Japan. The model was in the US.

Membrane roof celebrating 25 years

Early morning on June 28, 1987, air was blown throughout the arena, and the suspended membrane surface was gradually lifted. After 3 hours, it reached the designed height without any problem. The inflated membrane roof does not fit angular corners of a rectangular plan well. A special square shape plan with round corners was adopted. It is a so-called super ellipse.

1-3-61 Koraku, Bunkyo-ku, Tokyo
Architectural design / structural design: Nikken Sekkei, Takenaka Corporation
Construction: Takenaka Corporation, Taiyo Kogyo   Completion: 1988   Structure type: Low rise cable reinforced air membrane structure roof, RC structure, SRC structure (lower part)

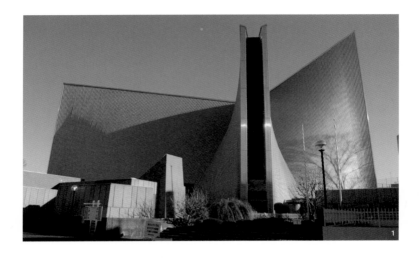

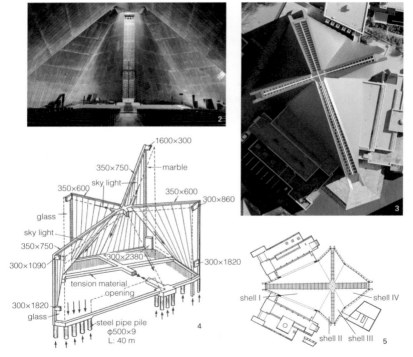

1 / General exterior view　2 / Interior view
3 / The cross shape crowned on the building is clearly observed from above
4 / Structural system　5 / Arrangement of shell elements.

St Mary's Cathedral

Sensationally elegant spatial modeling orchestrated by eight HP shells

Space like in the womb created by HP shell hipped roof

Along Mejiro-dori, there appears a modern sculptural building with brilliance of silver. People's eyes become glued to a strong sculptural beauty of this building. Eight HP shells of four types with stainless steel cladding rise up on a steep slope from the cathedral floor of a quadrilateral plan to the top to integrate a cross-shaped top light. This dramatic spatial composition also surrounds and creates a cathedral space like in the womb, inside. The visual impression given by its saddle-shaped curved surface of the HP shells evokes the suspended roofs of the Yoyogi National Stadium.

Although the structure of the compression type, shells (St Mary's Cathedral), completely differs from the tension type, suspended roofs (Yoyogi National Stadium), the architecture shares a common impression of Tange and Tsuboi's works during this period. It is a symbolic work that impresses that their works aimed at beauty with elegance, dynamism and tension, without falling into inorganic rigid rationalism.

Force flow design in eight shell walls

The boundaries of each shell are reinforced by edge beams, and pairs of edge beams facing each other are connected by short beams. Since the ends of the eight upper boundary beams gather in the center of the roof, these ends are firmly connected each other and a cross beam is also binding them in order to deal with the unbalanced axial force induced under a horizontal load. All shells are 12 centimeters thick stiffened by ribs in the vertical and horizontal directions at a pitch of about 2 meters. These ribs are not designed just to improve the out-of-plane flexural rigidity of the shell surface and reduce the bending moment due to eccentricity of the edge beams, but also to be used for attaching stainless roof claddings.

Since the largest shell I has a wide opening of 20 m for attached buildings, the outward thrust at the foot of the ridgeline with the adjacent shell II is designed so as to balance with the thrust of shells III and IV on the opposite side by tie beams installed under the ground floor.

3-16-5 Sekiguchi, Bunkyo-ku, Tokyo

Architectural design: Kenzo Tange + TANGE ASSOCIATES / Structural design: Yoshikatsu Tsuboi & Ryohei Nasukawa   Construction: Taisei Corporation   Completion: 1964

Major renovation: 2007   Structure type: Reinforced concrete shell construction

Chapter 7

Ueno & Sumida

027 The National Museum of Western Art, Main Building **P.96**
7-7 Ueno Park, Taito-ku, Tokyo

028 Tokyo Bunka Kaikan **P.98**
5-45 Ueno Park, Taito-ku, Tokyo

029 Tokyo National Museum Horyuji Treasures Museum **P.100**
13-9 Ueno Park, Taito-ku, Tokyo

google map

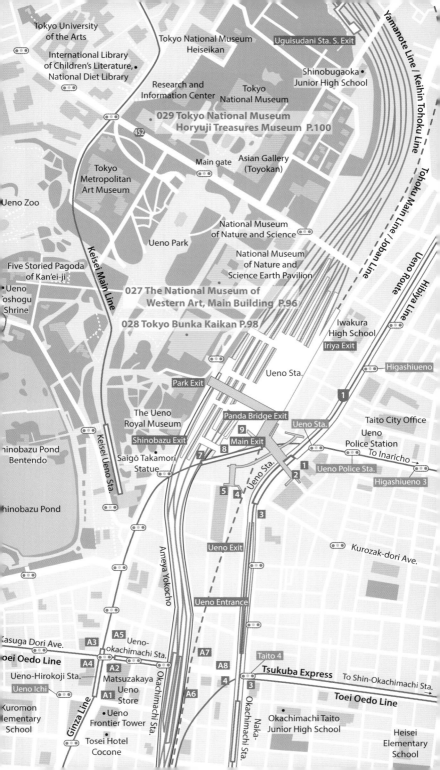

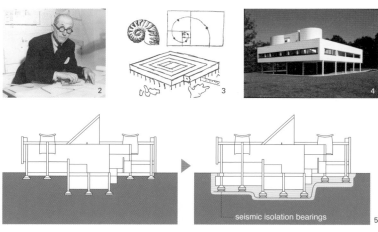

seismic isolation bearings

1 / View from the front yard
2 / Le Corbusier
3 / Museum of Unlimited Extension
4 / Villa Savoye(Poissy, France, 1931)
5 / Base Isolation Retrofit

Opening hours: 9: 30-17: 30, until 20:00 on Fridays
*Admission ends 30 minutes before closing time
Closed on: Mondays
(the following Tuesday if Monday is a holiday), New Year holidays
URL: http://www.nmwa.go.jp/

The National Museum of Western Art, Main Building

Seismic isolation devices protect the piloti structure

Piloti structure susceptible to earthquakes

The main building of the National Museum of Western Art (Fig. 1) is the only work of Le Corbusier (Fig. 2) in Japan, and reflects the concept of a "Museum of Unlimited Extension" that he advocated. According to this concept, the building may be expanded outwards infinitely like a snail (Fig. 3). The permanent exhibition route is also designed to follow a spiral path from the central "19th Century Hall" outwards.

Le Corbusier incorporated pilotis for the central hall, a structure frequently used in his works. Pilotis are slender columns that lift the building volume off the ground, freeing up the space underneath (Fig. 4). However, the piloti story is vulnerable to earthquakes. The low-rise buildings with short natural period have high seismic response, and concentrates the earthquake energy at this "soft story", which has caused collapse in past earthquakes.

Early example of base-isolation retrofit

In the 1990s, the seismic performance was re-evaluated and judged to be insufficient, requiring a seismic retrofit. However, conventional seismic retrofit methods such as (1) inserting concrete walls or steel braces between the pilotis or (2) wrapping the pilotis with concrete or steel plates risked ruining Le Corbusier's design intent. Therefore, it was decided to base isolate the main building using laminated rubber bearings (Fig. 5).

This improved the seismic performance while preserving the aesthetics of the original piloti superstructure.

Seismic isolation is also an effective retrofit strategy for "brittle" brick structures, and made possible the renovation of the Tokyo Station Marunouchi Building and reconstruction of the Mitsubishi Ichigokan.

The laminated rubber bearings are visible from a lounge window in the basement floor of the National Museum of Western Art.

7-7 Ueno Park, Taito-ku, Tokyo
Architectural design: Le Corbusier
Base Isolation Design & Supervision: Ministry of Construction, Kanto Regional Construction Bureau, Repair Department; Mayekawa Associates; Yokoyama Structural Architects
Structural design: Fugaku Yokoyama
Construction: Shimizu Corporation
Completion: 1959
Base Isolation Retrofit: 1998
Structure type: reinforced concrete structure

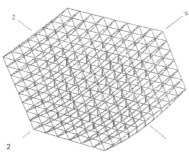

1 / Exterior of the building

2 / Main Hall roof. The roof has a hexagonal shape with a maximum height of 17 m. The structure comprises two lines of moment frame around the hall's perimeter. The walls and seating tiers are constructed in precast concrete. The 40 m roof spans were realized using parabolic trusses with the chords curved downwards, giving a convex ceiling shape that contributes to the hall acoustics.

3 / Cross section

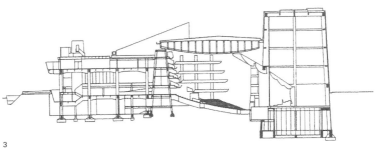

Tokyo Bunka Kaikan
Dynamic architecture with a simple structure

Japan's first international theater

This building is the work of Kunio Maekawa, a key figure in modern Japanese architecture. It faces the National Museum of Western Art, which was designed by Le Corbusier, Maekawa's teacher.

This was the first theater in Japan to systematically incorporate a rigorous acoustic design, and became the basis for the design of theatre halls in postwar Japan. Even after many renovations, the stunning quality of the sound still attracts visitors from all over the world.

Two halls and a foyer

As visitors pass under the curved eaves, they enter a wide open lobby with the ticket office. Continuing along with the restaurant above, the low ceiling gives way to a foyer with a high atrium. Ueno Park and the National Museum of Western Art are visible through large glass panes, and the wall of the Main Hall rises on the left. To the left of the foyer entrance is a gradual slope leading up to the smaller Recital Hall. Both the small and large halls are contained in one expansive space.

Structure based on ultimate strength theory

In addition to impressive architectural features, such as the curved eaves and louvers, numerous sculptors participated in the interior design. Most prominently, the sculptors Ryokichi Mukai and Masayuki Nagare contributed to the design of both halls, particularly in the acoustics. The structure was designed by the engineer Toshihiko Kimura, who adopted different structural systems appropriate for each hall and foyer. These were designed following what is hailed as the ultimate strength theory, where the connected structures are stronger than the individual parts.

The foyer is a reinforced concrete moment frame with encased steel sections, with both the columns and beams arranged on a 10.8 m square grid.

5-45 Ueno Park, Taito-ku, Tokyo
Architectural Design: Kunio Maekawa Architectural Design Office
Structural design: Yokoyama Architects
Acoustic design: Nagata Acoustic
Construction: Shimizu Corporation
Completion: 1961
Structure type: reinforced concrete structure, steel structure (roof)

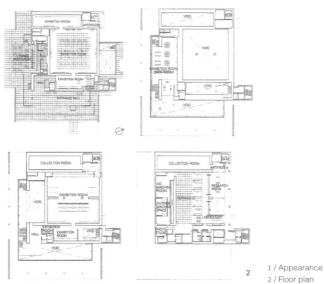

1 / Appearance
2 / Floor plan

TEL: 050-5541-8600
Opening hours: 9:30–17:00, admission until 16:30 *
* May vary depending on the season
Closed on: Mondays (closed on the following Tuesday if Monday is a national holiday), New Year holidays

Tokyo National Museum Horyuji Treasures Museum
Façade that supports the roof

Numerous expressions from only three elements

This building stands inconspicuously in a corner of Ueno Park, with its façade reflected in a pond situated in front of the entrance. The façade is comprised of a glass box with thin sashes framed by deep aluminum eaves. A thick limestone wall behind the glass contrasts with the delicate vertical grid and thin eaves. The glass box, encasing eaves and the limestone volume are arranged asymmetrically in a way which creates a sense of depth. By playing with the materials, light and proportions, this building has a myriad of "expressions" created by three simple elements.

Closed and open

The Gallery of Horyuji Treasures at the Tokyo National Museum is a facility for preserving and displaying more than 300 artifacts donated by the Horyuji temple to the Imperial family. These contrasting functions of permanent preservation and public exhibition simultaneously require both closedness and openness. The architect Yoshio Taniguchi solved the competing objectives with a simple geometric structure.

The storage facility and exhibition room must be protected to enable long term preservation. Therefore, these are housed in closed spaces constructed of concrete and stone, and located in the center of the building. Conversely, spaces that require openness, such as the lobby and lounge, are constructed with steel and glass, and are located along the perimeter.

Clear structural plan and attention to detail

The structure follows the architectural design concept, with the central storage and exhibition room made of reinforced concrete (RC), and the surrounding lobby and lounge made of steel. The central RC structure creates a closed space and acts as a core that resists the seismic load of the entire structure. As a result, the lobby roof is supported with slender steel columns that are subjected only to small gravity loads. The fine details and carefully weighed proportions create a sense of tension. The priceless treasures and exhibition pedestals are protected by seismic isolation devices installed at each individual display.

13-9 Ueno Park, Taito-ku, Tokyo
Architectural Design: Taniguchi Architectural Design Institute
Structural design: Kozo Keikaku Engineering
Construction: Obayashi Corporation
Completion: 1999
Structure type: reinforced concrete structure, steel structure

032 Sensō-ji Temple P.110

Hanayashiki

Umamichi

319

Sumida Park

Kototoibashi W.

Kototoibashi

Nitemmon

Nitenmon Gate

Taito City Citizens Center

6

Five-Story Pagoda of Sensō-ji

Hōzōmon Gate

Asakusa Elementary School

Higashisando

Dembōin

Asakusa 2

Sumida River

Sumida Pa

Matsuya

Nakamise

Asakusa Sta.

Shinakadori entrance

6

SHUTO EXPWY No.6 Mukojima Line

Sumida City Hall

Kaminarimon-dori St.

Kaminarimon Gate

8

5

Sumida City Office

Asakusa 1

Kaminarimon Gate 1

3

Azumabashi

Mitsui sumitomo bank

2

Asakusa culture Tourist Information center

A5

4

Azumabashi

461

A4

A3

Asakusa Sta.

6

Toei asakusa line

Ginza Line

463

Asakusa Sta.

Komagata 1

Komagata Bldg-W.

A

Asakusa fire station

A1

A2

Komagatabashi

453

Kiyosumi-dori Ave.

To Kuramae Sta.

Asakusa, Oshiage

google map

google map

Tokyo Skytree

Steel pipe truss structure with a central pillar vibration control mechanism made of prestressed concrete

Silhouette of "Sori(warp in)" and "Mukuri(warp out)"

Tokyo Skytree is a radio wave transmission tower designed for digital broadcasting communication of the metropolitan area, and has a height of 634 m, which is the highest in the world as a self-supporting transmission tower. This tower is the heart of the large-scale complex development consisting of facilities such as observation platform, shops, aquariums, dome theaters, office towers and district heating and cooling. The highly public role of the broadcasting business of the tower requires high structural performance so that it can maintain the main functions even after a major disaster. At the same time, a design which represents a new landmark not only of Tokyo but also of Japan was required. Its silhouette has two curves at its two corners, with a dignified tension, expressing the "Sori", warp of the Japanese sword, and the "Mukuri", warp out of the column in colonnades in Japanese temple architecture.

Structural design

In the structural design, a steel pipe lattice structure with triangular grids, contributing to express the silhouette of the tower, was adopted. The main members are steel pipes with round cross section, most flexible in joint processing and fitting to curved lines. The completion of the building required high-precision steel frame manufactur-ing, production, and construction techniques which have been cultivated in Japan.

Total repainting is scheduled for about every 20 years by using fluorine-based thick anticorrosion coat for the rust-preventive coating of steel frame members exposed outdoors and facilitating maintenance decks for complicated-joint parts where keeping coating quality for a long time is difficult.

400–600 MPa class steel for the main members reasonably reduced the weight of the tower for its extreme height.

Plan of foundation

The foundation directly supporting the tower has the same shape as the base and has steel reinforced concrete shear walls arranged along the sides of a regular triangle of about 70 m. They ensure the rigidity and strength of the foundation. Directly under the tripod truss, there are adopted "continuous pile-walls with knuckles", the pile-walls penetrated in the bearing stratum by about 15 m, to gain the higher resistance against up-lift.

Observation and setting design load of upper-air wind

Since design codes for 600 m–class high-rise structures had not yet been prepared, the design team have conducted upper-air wind observation using GPS Sonde to obtain necessary data, and completed the structural

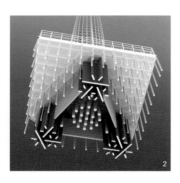

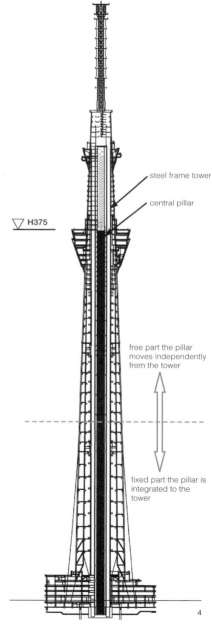

steel frame tower

central pillar

▽ H375

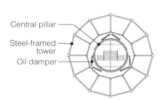

Central pillar
Steel-framed tower
Oil damper

Connection by dampers

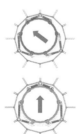

**Various movements absorbed
by dampers**

⬅ movement of pillar

free part the pillar
moves independently
frem the tower

fixed part the pillar is
integrated to the
tower

3

4

design for wind load.

This design method and data can be regarded as a study for 1,000 m class super high-rise building design in Japan, that can be well used in the future.

Shimbashira, the central pillar, vibration control mechanism

The evacuation staircase of the tower is a tubular prestressed concrete structure, and is utilized as the central pillar, which associates with the newly developed and adopted vibration control system for reducing structural resonance stimulated by earthquakes or wind loads. Since the function of the center pillar in the system reminds "Shimbashira", central pillars in traditional pagodas in Japanese Buddhism Temples, then it was so named. The height of the Shimbashira is 375 m, and was designed to have a slightly longer natural period than that of the steel-framed tower, so that it gives a similar effect as a mass damper to the tower. It has a fixed part and a free part along the height of the tower. The fixed part is integrated with the steel-frame of the tower and a free part can move independently. Oil dampers are equipped in the free part and control the relative displacement between the steel-frame and the Shimbashira. The shaking re-

duction of the Shimbashira mechanism is effective for various types of earthquakes such as long-period earthquakes or epicentral earthquakes of short-period, and can reduce a maximum of 50% during earthquakes and a maximum of 30% during strong winds comparing to the response of a non-vibration controlled tower.

1 / General view of the east side
2 / Schematic view of the foundation
3–4 / Concept of shimbashira vibration control
5 / Different silhouettes of the tower

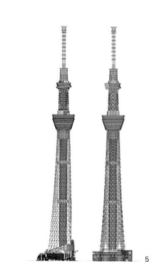

5

1-1-13 Oshiage, Sumida-ku, Tokyo
Architectural design: Nikken Sekkei Ltd. (Shigeru Yoshino, Tetsuo Tsuchiya)
Structural design: Nikken Sekkei Ltd.
(Atsuo Konishi, Kazunari Watanabe. Norio Nakanishi, Yoshisato Esaka)
Construction: Obayashi Corporation
Completion: 2012
Structure type: Steel construction (Tower body)
Prestressed concrete construction (Shimbashira column)
Foundation: Steel reinforced concrete wall pile foundation work (Directly below the tower)

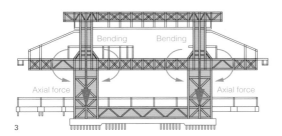

1 / Exterior view
2 / During construction
3 / Schematic drawing of the
skeleton

Edo-Tokyo Museum
Super skeleton with four mega columns and two girders

Piloti and Metabolism

On the east side of the Sumida River, next to the Ryogoku Kokugikan, Sumo wrestling arena, there is a building standing with a unique configuration. The architectural design resembling a giant temple or Japanese stilt warehouse, is by Kiyonori Kikutake, who led the "Metabolism" movement in 1970's, and the structural design is by Gengo Matsui. The height is 62 m, which is identical to the height of the Edo Castle tower, a skyscraper built with timber construction 400 years ago. All spatial complexes are supported by a structural system composed of a main super skeleton and secondary sub-structures. This structural composition is designed so that the main space can accommodate the change of demand through time, and this approach corresponds to the philosophy of Metabolism.

Four mega columns and girders supporting the upper space

The structure is strong and simple. The four huge columns that support the upper space are connected at the top and bottom by rigid girders. The longitudinal frame that receives small beams sticks out as cantilevers so that the bending moments are balanced between the girders and only the axial force is induced to the columns (Fig. 3). The permanent axial load per column is approximately 25,000 ft. This axial force is transmitted to the mat-like foundation supported by 100 piles through a mega column of H-shape with an outer dimension of 14.4 m.

Seismic design by rigid structure +damping

In order to suppress horizontal deformation during earthquakes, a rigid structure was designed, having a primary natural frequency of 1.2–1.5 Hz, which does not coincide with the frequency of earthquake tremor.

In addition, in order to avoid excessive vertical movement of the cantilever which may damage exhibits, 126 vertical vibration damping devices are equipped in the double floor at the tip of the cantilever, and, as the result, the vertical movement during large earthquakes is reduced to about 1/4.

The total weight of the steel used for the frame is about 23,000 t. Pay a visit and appreciate the special structure featuring 43 m notable overhangs.

1-4-1 Yokoami, Sumida-ku, Tokyo
Architectural Design: Kiyonori Kikutake Architects
Structural design: Gengo Matsui + O.R.S.office
Construction: Kajima Construction and other 8 consortium
Completion: 1993
Structure type: Steel structure

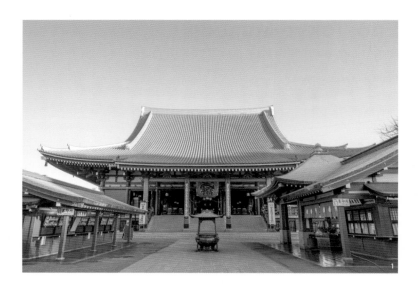

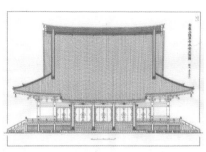

1 / Exterior of Sensoji Main Hall
2 / Elevation view of the main hall of Sensoji Temple
3 / Formwork for the roof
4 / Model of Ryounkaku

Sensoji Temple and Asakusa Towers
Downtown landmark

Sensoji main hall

The current main hall is a reconstruction of an original that burned down in 1945, and is the first work of the famous shrine and temple architect Minoru Ooka (1900–1987). Funded through public donations, there was consideration that "religious buildings built on the public's purse should avoid timber construction due to the fire risks." Yet at the same time, there was a strong desire to maintain the appearance of the original, and so the traditional timber shrine style was adopted. This was the first traditional timber building reproduced in steel reinforced concrete (SRC), which refers to steel sections encased in reinforced concrete. Changing the structural material while maintaining the aesthetics posed some challenges and required a combination of primary structural SRC and ornamental timber.

The traditional Hijiki bracket was retained, but treated as a nonstructural load, as small RC members provide little structural function. A constriction shape of the traditional column capital is a disadvantage to an RC column; therefore, a Daibutsu (Big Buddha)-style capital with less constriction was applied. Seismic retrofit was also carried out in 2006 and 2010, enhancing the strength through the provision of RC shear walls at the four corners, and reducing the seismic mass by replacing the heavy Japanese roof tiles with lightweight titanium roofing.

Asakusa towers

The Asakusa neighborhood features many towers, from the Sensoji Temple's 5-story pagoda to the Tokyo Skytree. Two notable towers, the Ryounkaku and Jintan tower, were also located in this area but no longer exist. Ryounkaku was a pioneering 12-story brick masonry building built in 1890, and was one of the first high-rise buildings in Tokyo. However, unreinforced masonry tends to perform poorly in earthquakes, and the upper stories collapsed during the 1923 Great Kanto Earthquake, leading to its subsequent demolition. It was then imitated in reconstruction as the Jintan tower, which was also demolished in 1986 due to aging.

2-3-1 Asakusa, Taito-ku, Tokyo
Architectural Design: Minoru Ooka Building Research Institute
Completion: 1956
Seismic retrofit: 2010

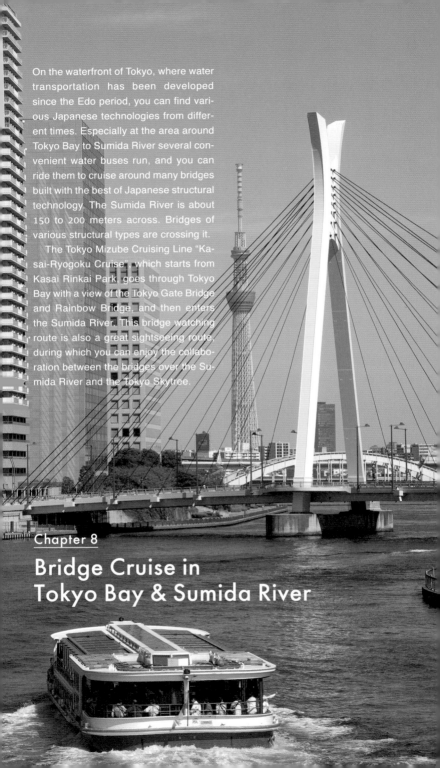

On the waterfront of Tokyo, where water transportation has been developed since the Edo period, you can find various Japanese technologies from different times. Especially at the area around Tokyo Bay to Sumida River several convenient water buses run, and you can ride them to cruise around many bridges built with the best of Japanese structural technology. The Sumida River is about 150 to 200 meters across. Bridges of various structural types are crossing it.

The Tokyo Mizube Cruising Line "Kasai-Ryogoku Cruise" which starts from Kasai Rinkai Park, goes through Tokyo Bay with a view of the Tokyo Gate Bridge and Rainbow Bridge, and then enters the Sumida River. This bridge watching route is also a great sightseeing route, during which you can enjoy the collaboration between the bridges over the Sumida River and the Tokyo Skytree.

Chapter 8
Bridge Cruise in Tokyo Bay & Sumida River

Structural form of a bridge

A bridge is an "aerial route" that connects two distant points across a river or valley. Since ancient times, various types of structures have been tested in order to create aerial routes for people, cars, and trains over long distances against gravity.

The following is an overview of basic types of structures: beam (bending), arch (compression), and suspension (tension) types. Besides them, there are also truss, rahmen bridges, various movable, and floating type of bridges. For the material of bridges, starting from selections in nature, plants, wood, and stone, various industrialized materials were applied; iron, steel, RC, FRP and so on. Bridges have been replaced not only due to decrepitude but also being destroyed by wars or disasters.

Each bridge also tells a history of people's lives.

Girder bridge

The most basic component of the bridge is the girder. A girder is often referred as a "beam" in structural mechanics. The beam is one of the simplest structural elements, but it is difficult to utilize the full strength of the material because stress distribution is not uniform in the section, reaching maximum at the edges in the direction of its depth due to "bending moment". For this inefficiency, it cannot be used for very large spans. By increasing the depth, distance between upper and lower edges or strengthening the critical parts, beam type bridges can be applied for larger spans to some extent but normally it is limited to around 100m span.

Cantilever
For a bridge, a set of two cantilever beams overhanging from both sides to meet in the middle of the span are employed.

In a cantilever beam, the bending moment reaches its maximum at the support point. Therefore thick strong structure is required at each side.

Simple beam
The simplest form of a bridge. Since the maximum bending moment occurs at the center, the central part must be made strong.

Continuous Beam
Although it looks simple, its stress distribution is not simple. Secondary stresses developed due to settlement of support and variation of temperature, and requires careful calculation and design.

Gerber beam
The stress state is relatively simple, and the bending moment is maximum at the bridge pier and zero at support points. Since it can flexibly accomodate thermal expansion and contraction, and ground subsidence, design and calculation are relatively simple.

* Please check the water bus routes by yourself since they may be changed occasionally.

Arch bridge

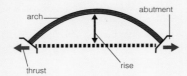

By arching up the center of a beam, the bending moment is drastically diminished and force in the member can be transmitted mostly as compression. This system is called an arch. Since the force is transmitted as compression uniformly in the member section, the full strength of the material can be used.

Since a couple of large horizontal force (thrust) occurs at the support points, strong structures are required there. Although compressive stress is dominant in the structure, it is necessary to add some bending rigidity to the arch ribs to prepare for possible large load fluctuations. The arch system is often applied to spans up to about 500 m.

Deck-type arch

Deck arch does not have structures above the deck and is often selected when the bridge is designed to provide a wide open view on the deck. On the other hand, structures beneath the deck may be affected in the case of flood.

Therefore the bridge should be constructed high enough above the river. By widening the arch width, it can take strong lateral wind.

Through-type arch

The main structure is an arch, and for the through arch type, the deck structure can be used as a tie that takes the thrust force.

This structure is often called "tied arch." Its self-equilibrated (self-balancing) system does not require any heavy structure against the thrust force at the support point.

Half-through-type arch

The deck structure passes through the middle height of the arch. The height of the road surface and its structure can be chosen to some extent. By making the arch width wider than the roads, crosswinds can be resisted effectively. The mixture of landscape and skeletons can create interesting visual variations.

Langer bridge

The main structure is the beam (stiffening girder) that holds the road. The arch supports the beam and takes its load and transmits to both ends as a compressive force. The thrust is canceled by the axial force of the stiffening girders at the ends. The arch is thin and polygonal with straight members because it is expected to transmit only axial force and no bending.

A bridge in which both the arch and the stiffening girder have bending rigidity is called a "Lohse bridge."

Suspension bridges

Suspension bridge is a structural type of bridge in which the bridge beams are hung from a pair of tension-resistant cables that are suspended between two high places (such as tops of main towers) at both sides of main span. A bridge that suspends the bridge girders directly from main towers without main cables is called a "cable-stayed bridge".

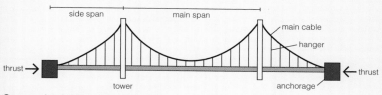

Suspension bridge (suspension type)

The bridge decks are suspended by hangers from the main cables passed between the towers. Large structures (anchorages) are required at the end of the main cables to restrain the thrust due to strong tension of the main cable. The shape and rigidity of deck-girders are designed to be stable against wind based on aero-dynamics.

A suspension bridge is a type of bridge that can allow the longest span with current technology, and it is possible to span about up to 2 km.

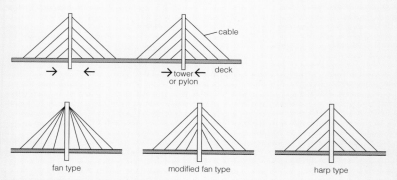

Cable-stayed bridge (cable-stayed type)

In this type, the bridge decks are directly suspended from the main towers by diagonal cables. Since cables are arranged diagonally, horizontal compressive forces toward the main tower act on the decks and this force is symmetrically balanced at the main tower. As a result, this type is a self-anchored structure in which the decks transmit compressive forces. This type is suitable for bridges from 100 m to 1 km.

The axial force of the girders and the stability of the main tower vary depending on the arrangement of cables, and the visual impressions are also different.

Senju-ohashi Bridge

Suijin-ohashi Bridge

Shirahige Bridge

Kototoi Bridge

16. Azuma Bridge

Higashi-Mukojima Sta.

Sensoji Temple P.110

Sakura Bridge

Hikifune Sta.

Asakusa Nitenmon

Asakusa Sta.

Oshiage Sta.

Tokyo Skytree P.104

Asakusa Tourist Information Center

Tokyo Skytree Sta.

Ryogoku River Center

15. Komagata Bridge

13. Kuramae Bridge

14. Umaya Bridge

Ryogoku Kokugikan

Ryogoku Sta.

Kinshichō Sta.

12. Sumidagawa Bridge

Edo-Tokyo Museum P.108

Kyunaka River

Arakawa River

11. Ryogoku Bridge

10. Shin-ohashi Bridge

Imperial Palace

Onagi River

9. Kiyosu Bridge

Tokyo Sta.

Kiba Park

6. Chuo-ohashi Bridge

8. Sumidagawa-ohashi Bridge

7. Eitai Bridge

Shimbashi Sta.

Shiodome Sta.

5. Tsukuda-ohashi Bridge

4. Kachidoki Bridge

Waters Takeshiba

Toyosu Sta.

Tokyo Aquatics Centre P.16

3. Tsukiji-ohashi Bridge

Shin-Toyosu Sta.

Ariake Arena P.20

Shin-Kiba Sta.

Tamachi Sta.

Kasai Rinkai Park

Shinonome Sta.

Shinagawa Sta.

2. Rainbow Bridge

Ariake Gymnastics Centre P.18

Kokusai-Tenjijō Sta.

Kasai Seaside Park Rest House P.134

Kasai Rinkai Park

Daiba Sta.

Tokyo Big Sight P.130

Wakasu Seaside Park

Fuji Television Headquarters Building (FCG Building) P.132

1. Tokyo Gate Bridge

1. Tokyo Gate Bridge

Looking like two dinosaurs facing each other, this huge truss bridge spans the Tokyo Port Waterfront Road over the Third Sea Route between Wakasu and the reclaimed land outside the Central Breakwater. Due to the conditions of airspace restrictions at Haneda Airport (height 98.1 m or less) and sea route restrictions on the Third Sea Route (route width 300 m, height 54.6 m), the height of this bridge was designed as 87.8 m. The structure is a mixed structure of steel truss and floor box girder, and it provides a dramatic visual sequence in the relationships of the structure, road surface and landscape of sea. The road surface passes from deck, half-through to through type areas, and finally reaches the open central part with the box girder. The trusses are all welded on site to make the joints compact, and the floor slabs are integrated with the structural members to reduce the concavity and convexity of the outer surfaces of the members, thereby improving maintainability, durability, and artistic design. In the lower road part, upper cross members were reduced to reserve better visibility and landscape for the users.

Completion: February 12, 2012, Bridge part length: 760 m (2618 m: including approach) Main span: 440 m, Box beam span: 120 m, Width: 24.0 m, Structure: Steel, 3-span continuous truss and box composite

2. Rainbow Bridge

The white symbol of Tokyo Bay is now nearly 30 years old. This is a suspension bridge as a transportation complex in which the Highway No. 11 Daiba Line, seaside road (Seaside Aomi Line), and Tokyo Waterfront New Transit (Yurikamome) connect Shibaura Wharf and No. 6 Daiba and straddle the First Route of Tokyo Bay. It was designed under the airspace restriction of Haneda Airport (height less than 150 m) and the sea route restriction of the Third Route (passage width 500 m, height 50 m). The main cable of the central span is a bundle of 127 strands, consisting of 127 galvanized steel wires (5.37 mm diameter), respectively. Four hanger ropes with a diameter of 68 mm are used at each hanging point. In 2013, the main cables were repainted. The suspended double-deck stiffening girders are 8.9m high and 29 m wide, straight chord Warren truss in the longitudinal direction and K-truss in the transverse direction.

Since the foundations of the huge main tower and the anchorage on the Daiba side are underwater, the pneumatic caisson method, in which a sealed working caisson is sunk and compressed air is sent to create an airtight working space, was used. There is a promenade at the lower level of the double deck for pedestrians.

Completion: August 26, 1993, Bridge part length: 798 m (3750 m: including approach) Central span: 570 m, Side span: 147.5 m, Sag: 57.6 m (sag ratio: about 1/10) Main tower height: 126 m, Width: 29.0 m, Structure: 3-span 2-hinge suspension bridge (double deck stiffened truss)

3. Tsukiji-ohashi Bridge

This new bridge constructed at the place where Loop Line No.2 crosses the Sumida River and connects the city center and waterfront area where Olympic Village of Tokyo 2021 was alocated. The bridge has an open appearance by tilting the arches outward to eliminate the transversal supports passing over. Both the central and side spans were erected by a large block construction method. The tied arch of the central span (120 m long, 18 m high, 2600 tons weight) was transported and constructed by a huge crane ship on May 8, 2014.

Completion: November 2018, Total length: 245m, Width: 32.3-48.0m, Central span: 145m, Side span: 50m, Structure: Steel 3-span half-through arch, Steel shell caisson (bridge pier)

4. Kachidoki Bridge

This is the only Chicago-type double-leaf bascule bridge in Japan, which was constructed for Tsukishima Expo 1940 (canceled). The bridge once had been operated to open the water passage when necessary, but due to the increase in traffic on land, it has been closed for water passage since 1970. The Chicago type is a cantilever bridge with a shaft and a large gear at the support. The bridge opens by turning the gear with a motor. The Kachidoki Bridge has a pair of these structures facing each other and opens up to 70 degrees. The side spans through a tied-arch structure.

Completion: June 14, 1940, Total length: 246 m, Width: 22 m, Maximum fulcrum distance: 51.6 m (movable part), 86.0 m (fixed part), Structure: RC (abutment, bridge pier), Chicago-type double-leaf bascule bridge (central part), Through-type tied arch (side span)

5. Tsukuda-ohashi Bridge

This is the first post-war bridge built over the Sumida River in preparation for the Tokyo Olympic games in 1964. This bridge symbolizes Japan's high growth period, which prioritized function without decoration. It is not orthogonal but tilted 62 degrees to the shore. A large block of the bridge, 44m long, 155 tons were assembled at the IHI Tsukudajima factory, and then towed by marine crane to be set in place. The steel weight is 2246 tons (408 kgw/m^2).

Completion: August 27, 1964, Total length: 222 m Width: 25.2 m Structure: Continuous 3-span steel box girder with decks

6. Chuo-ohashi Bridge

A fan-type cable-stayed bridge suspended by 32 cables, designed in consideration of the urban landscape. The road curves at the foot of main tower. The tower top is designed in the shape of Kabuto (Samurai helmet), in reference to the fact that the eastern bank, Ishikawajima Island, was once called Yoroijima (Armor Island).

Completion: August 26, 1993, Total length: 210.7 m Width: 25.0 m Structure: Continuous 2-span cable-stayed with steel decks

7. Eitai Bridge

This is the first bridge built in the Great Kanto Earthquake reconstruction project. It was modeled after the Ludendorff Bridge in Germany (collapsed during the war) with a masculine design of a compression arch. The steel weight is 3932 tons (965 kgw/m^2). The first bridge was built in 1698. The steel bridge built in 1897 collapsed in the fire after the Great Kanto Earthquake.

Ladder-shaped Toyomi Bridge (1927, Vierendeel Bridge) can be seen at the mouth of Nihonbashi River on the west side just upstream of the Eitai Bridge.

Completion: December 20, 1926, Bridge length: 184.7 m Width: 25.0 m Structure: Central span: Through tied-arch, Side span: Steel girder

8. Sumidagawa-ohashi Bridge

A two-story bridge built for the construction of the Metropolitan Expressway No. 9 Fukagawa Line. The upper part is the elevated bridge for the Metropolitan Expressway (steel weight: 2743 tons), and the lower part is for Ningyocho Street (Suitengu-dori), separately called Sumidagawa-ohashi Bridge (steel weight 2466 t). It has very few points to be mentioned from the landscape point of view.

Completion: October 1979, River section total length: 210.0 m, Width: 30.0 m, Mains span: continuous 3-span steel box girder with decks, Side span: Simple composite girder, Elevated part: simple PC girder

9. Kiyosu Bridge

This bridge is a self-equilibrated suspension bridge that was built as a part of the Great Kanto Earthquake Recovery Project and was called the "bell of the Recovery". The graceful design of a suspension bridge, following the Hindenburg Bridge in Cologne, Germany (destroyed during the war), was planned to make a good contrast with the masculine design of Eitai Bridge. Three bridges, Kachidoki, Eitai, and Kiyosu, were designated as National Important Cultural Properties in 2007.

Completion: March 1928, Bridge length: 186.3 m, Width: 22.0 m, Structure: Self-anchored steel suspension bridge

10. Shin-ohashi Bridge

The first Shin-ohashi Bridge was built in 1693. It was built as the third bridge after the Senju and Ryogoku bridges. This bridge is depicted in Utagawa Hiroshige's famous Ukiyoe. print, "Ohashi Atake no Yudachi" (Sudden Shower at Ohashi Bridge and Atake area)*. The old bridge (1912) was the first steel truss bridge in Japan that survived and served as an evacuation route in the Great Kanto Earthquake and air raids in the World War II. It has been partially moved, reconstructed and exhibited at the Museum Meiji-mura in Aichi prefecture. The current Shin-ohashi Bridge is a harp-type cable-stayed bridge suspended by eight

cables that was rebuilt in 1977. It was designed in a simpler manner than the Chuo-ohashi Bridge constructed later.

Completion: March 27, 1977, Bridge length: 170.0 m, Width: 24.0 m, Structure: 2-span continuous cable-stayed bridge

11. Ryogoku Bridge

Learning from the fact people could not cross the river during the great Meireki fire in 1657, the bridge was built in 1661. Since the bridge connected two provinces, Musashi and Shimofusa, it was named Ryogoku, two provinces, Bridge. It accelerated the expansion of Edo city to the east. After the Great Kanto Earthquake, the old bridge (1904, 3-span arched Pratt truss iron bridge) was replaced with a steel plate girder Gerber bridge. On the bridge, there are decorations related to Sumo, fireworks and Art Déco style motifs. A span of the old bridge is re-used as the Minamitaka Bridge

over the Kamejima River, which joins Sumida River below the Chuo-Ohashi Bridge.

Completion: November 1932, Bridge length: 164.5 m Width: 24.0 m Structure: 3-span Gerber type steel plate girder

12. Sumidagawa Bridge

This bridge is a through type Langer girder bridge built for the purpose of extending the Sobu Main Line from Ryogoku Station to Ochanomizu Station.

Completion: March 1932, Bridge length: 172.0 m, Structure: 3-span through-type Gerber and Langer type girder

13. Kuramae Bridge

This is a deck-type arch iron bridge built as part of the Great Kanto Earthquake reconstruction project. Before its construction in the area, there was a ferry service, "Fujimi no Watashi", across the Sumida River. The name Kuramae, meaning "in front of storehouse", came from the fact that there was a rice storehouse of the Edo government on the right bank. Since sumo games were held at Kuramae Kokugikan gymnasium until 1984, there are decorations on the bridge with the motif of sumo wrestling and yakatabune (houseboats).

Completion: November 1927, Bridge length: 173. 2 m, Span: 50.902 m (maximum steel arch span), 12.192 m (concrete arch span), Width: 22.0 m, Structure: deck-type, 3-span continuous 2 hinge arch and deck-type fixed concrete arch

14. Umaya Bridge

The first bridge was built in 1874. The previous bridge (1893, Pratt truss iron bridge) was heavily damaged by fire after the Great Kanto Earthquake. The current bridge is a through-type tied arch bridge newly built as part of the earthquake reconstruction plan. The name comes from the fact that there was a stable for the rice storehouse of the Edo-government in the area. On the bridge, there are decorations of horses.

Completion: September 1929, Bridge length: 151.4 m Width: 22.0 m Structure: 3-span through-type tied-arch

* Sudden Shower over Shin Ohashi Bridge and Atake, from the Series One Hundred Scenic Spots of Edo

15. Komagata Bridge

This is an arch bridge newly built as part of the reconstruction plan after the Great Kanto Earthquake. The structures are deck-type arches in both side spans and a half-through-type arch in the center span. There was a ferry service, "Komagata no Watashi", across the Sumida River. The name comes from "Komagatado", a small Buddhism hall, on the right bank.

Completion: June 25, 1927, Bridge length: 149.6 m, Width: 22.0 m, Structure: Half-through type tied arch (center span), Deck-type arch (side span)

Sumo Wrestling and Kokugikan Stadium

16. Azuma Bridge

The first bridge was built in 1774. The former Pratt truss iron bridge (1887) was damaged by the fire immediately after the Great Kanto Earthquake. In 1931, it was replaced with a 3-span deck-type arch as part of the earthquake reconstruction project.

Completion: June 1931, Bridge length: 150.0 m, Width: 20.0 m, Structure: 3-span deck-type arch

History

Sumo is Japanese traditional wrestling performed in a 4.5 meter round ring called a "Dohyo" on a stage, which is made of clay. Sumo was originally a Shinto ritual for successful harvests and had been performed in many districts in Japan. It gradually became a spectacle for the public in the Edo period. The matches performed regularly at Ekoin Temple at Honjo in Tokyo were particularly popular. They needed a place free from weather conditions and decided to build a big roofed arena. It was architecturally designed by Kingo Tatsuno and Manji Kasai, who designed Tokyo Station. Structural design was by Toshikata Sano. This was the first Japanese big dome arena, Sumo Josetsu Kan, a permanent roofed stadium for Sumo, completed in 1909. The dome had a round plan with 62m diameter and 25m in height, constructed as a radial ribbed dome with truss arches, and could host 13,000 spectators. A glass glazed top light at the center shined the radial steel frames and the arena was nicknamed "A Great Steel Umbrella". The stadium was called "Kokugikan" that means "Stadium for National Sports", although there are no formal national sports in Japan even today. The stadium was unfortunately burned by an accidental fire in 1917. It was rebuilt in 1920 with a concrete cover. However, it was burned again by fire after the Kanto Earthquake in 1923. It was rebuilt again but burned again by the Tokyo Air Raid in 1945. Then it moved its place around from Hamacho and Kuramae, and finally reached Ryogoku to settle down in the current arena completed in 1984.

Design of Skeletons

For the structural design of the current Sumo Arena, Ryougoku Kokugikan Stadium, the skeleton of the original stadium, "A Great Steel Umbrella", was in the basic image of tradition. Eight big girders of 2.5m depth are radially arranged and tied by octagonal rings circumferentially. Bearing points were designed so that the points can slide radially under thermal deformation or other loads. The roof plane is mostly constructed by double-warren trusses of which members are assembled with cut-T steel members so that they show their sharp edges in interior appearance of the roof, in contrast with thick surfaces of eight big girders.

1 / Spectators in the first Kokugikan
2 / Ukiyoe print of Sumo wrestling

Chapter 9

Tokyo Bay Area

Tokyo Big Sight
Fuji Television Headquarters Building (FCG Building)
Shin-toyosu Brillia Running Stadium
Kasai Seaside Park Rest House

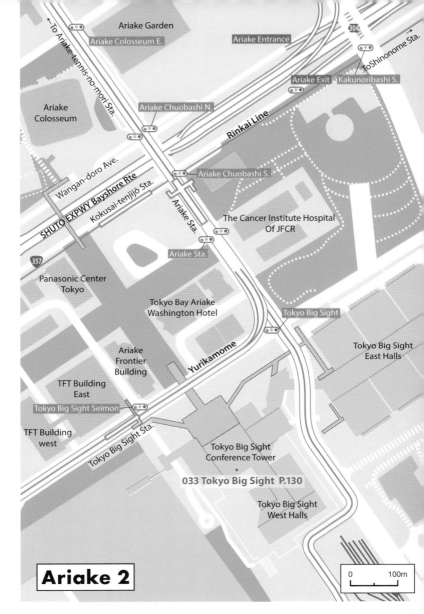

Ariake Garden

Ariake Colosseum E.

Ariake Entrance

304

←To Ariake-tennis-no-mori Sta.

ToShinonome Sta.→

Ariake Exit

Kakunoribashi S.

Ariake
Colosseum

Ariake Chuobashi N.

Rinkai Line

Wangan-doro Ave.

SHUTO EXPWY Bayshore Rte

Kokusai-tenjijō Sta.

Ariake Chuobashi S.

Ariake Sta.

The Cancer Institute Hospital
Of JFCR

357

Ariake Sta.

Panasonic Center
Tokyo

Tokyo Bay Ariake
Washington Hotel

Tokyo Big Sight

Tokyo Big Sight
East Halls

Yurikamome

Ariake
Frontier
Building

TFT Building
East

Tokyo Big Sight Seimon

TFT Building
west

Tokyo Big Sight Sta.

Tokyo Big Sight
Conference Tower

033 Tokyo Big Sight P.130

Tokyo Big Sight
West Halls

Ariake 2

0   100m

033 Tokyo Big Sight **P.130**
3-11-1 Ariake, Koto-ku, Tokyo

google map

034 Fuji Television Headquarters Building
(FCG Building) **P.132**

2-4-8 Daiba, Minato-ku, Tokyo

google map

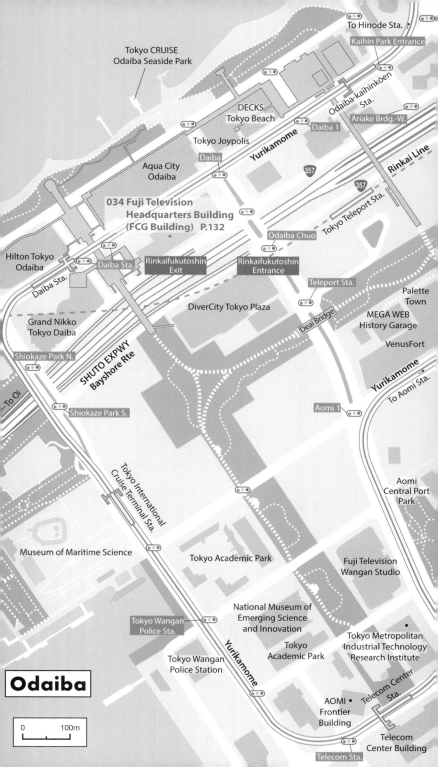

035 Shin-toyosu Brillia Running Stadium P.133 •

To Kachidoki Sta. →

SHUTO EXPWY No.10 Harumi Line

Harumi Bridge

← To Harumi area

Kanni-dori Ave.

Toyosu Ohashi Bridge

Shin-Toyosu Sta.

Harumiohashi minamizume

TEPCO Toyosu Building

IHI Stage Around Tokyo

Hotel JAL City Tokyo Toyosu

Yurikamome Line

Toyosu Exit

Toyosu Roku-chome Park

Shijō-mae Sta.

Ariake-dori Ave.

Toyosu Entrance

Toyosu Market Fruit and vegetable Building

To Shinonome JCT

Toyosu Market Fisheries Intermediate Wholesale Market Building

Toyosu Market Fisherise Wholesale Market Building

Ariake Gymnastic Center

Shinonome Canal

Ariake-Tennis-no-mori Sta.

Ariake Urban Sports Park

To Tokyo Big Sight

0   100m

Shin-Toyosu

035 Shin-toyosu Brillia Running Stadium   **P.133**

6-9-1 Toyosu, Koto-ku, Tokyo

google map

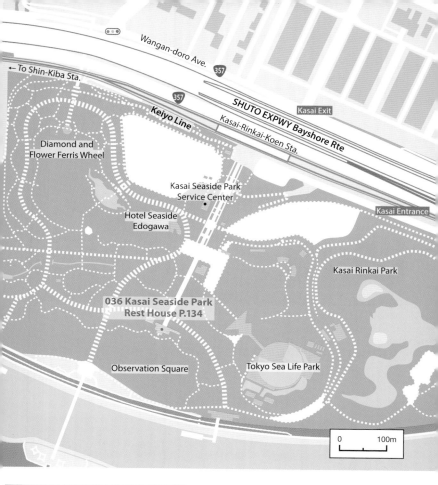

Kasai Seaside Park

036 Kasai Seaside Park Rest House **P.134**
6-2-3 Rinkaicho, Edogawa-ku, Tokyo

google map

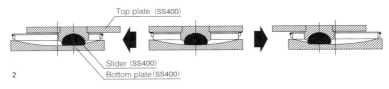

Top plate（SS400）

Slider（SS400）
Bottom plate（SS400）

2

3

4

5

1 / Congress Tower
2 / Schematic diagram of friction pendulum
　　bearing for Galleria
3–4 / Lift-up of the Congress Tower
5 / Interior view of a hall

Tokyo Big Sight
Huge conference complex with conbox system

Conbox system

This is a huge convention complex, consisting of exhibition halls and conference halls with area of over 80,000 m². The complex is commonly called as Tokyo Big Sight. Since the site is located in a newly developed waterfront city, the complex is designed as a collection of various images associated with sea, aiming to be an architecture creating a new landscape.

Huge hall area is divided by 45 m square grid system and a 6 m square structure called "conbox", in which the structure and equipment are integrated, placed at each intersection of the grid.

In the respect of structural design, the expansion joints required for long buildings are commonly laid out with conboxes, for the consistency with the planning design. Diagonally arranged spatial grid trusses support 45m distance between conboxes. At the place where the maximum span is 90m, a set of keel trusses, arranged at an angle of 45-degree, reduces the span to 64 m (45 m × √2), as a rational structural solution (Fig.5).

Galleria

Galleria has glass roofs with total length about 270 m. The thermal deformation of the steel skeleton and excessive deformation due to earthquakes or strong winds must be considered. In order to isolate the glass surface from these structural deformations, friction pendulums are adapted for bearings, and certain clearances are provided between the supporting structures and architectural finishes.

Congress Tower

The most striking part of the complex is the Congress Tower with a height about 60 m. The four assembled columns with side length of 9 m, are arranged following the grid of the conbox system,. The assembled columns support a conference hall with a huge dimension of 90 m × 90 m in pan. A gate-shaped superstructure is constructed on the upper part of the frame with three layers beam height, put on the four assembled columns. To support the overhanging upper floor, brace members are arranged at the edges of the inverted pyramids. During the construction of this huge plane, the lift-up procedure was efficiently adapted.

3-11-1 Ariake, Koto-ku, Tokyo
Architectural design: AXS SATOW INC.
Structural design: AXS SATOW INC. & ORIMOTO STRUCTURAL ENGINEERS
Construction: HAZAMA CORPORATE & AOKI CORPORATE joined venture
Completion: 1995
Structure type: Steel structure, Steel reinforced concrete structure,
Reinforced concrete structure

Fuji Television Headquarters Building (FCG Building)

Mega frame by Vierendeel girder

This is a signature building of the area with a sphere between the twin towers, which you can see when crossing the Rainbow Bridge from the inner-city area to Odaiba artificial island. The 25-story twin towers are connected by aerial corridors arranged in every 6 floors, and a sphere floats in the upper space of these corridors. Its form and appearance are recognized as an iconic design.

The basis of the structure is a so-called mega frame combined with assembled columns (3.2 × 4.8 m) with four pillars integrated by short-span beams, and assembled girders with two layers of floor beams. High-rise twin towers are composed of this basic frame system, and the two buildings are connected by a Vierendeel beam of

appropriate rigidity and strength to make the entire frame earthquake and gale resistant. The arch dome skeleton of the sphere is incorporated into this column as well as the Vierendeel beam. The overall exterior design directly expresses the structural system of the building.

2-4-8 Daiba, Minato-ku, Tokyo
Architectural design: TANGE ASSOCIATES
Structural design: KOBORI RESEACH COMPLEX INC.
Construction: KAJIMA CORPORATION
Completion: 1996
Structure type:
Aboveground part: Steel and partially steel reinforced concrete
Underground part: Reinforced concrete

Shin-toyosu Brillia Running Stadium

Long roof with ETFE cushions for Paralympians

Design concept of the facility is "sports x art" and its function is for top athletes with disabilities, such as Paralympians. The training center roof measures 108 meters by length, 16.3 m in width, 8.5 meters in height and houses a 60-meter track. The roofing is consisted of pillow-type cushions of ETFE foil with regulated inner pressure, enhancing resistance of cushions to snow and wind. The printing on the surface of ETFE foil controls the light transmission to 35% and lowers heat penetration, whilst maintaining a bright and open interior space. The roof frame is a hybrid structure, consisting of a steel arch frame and curved laminated timber beams, which stiffens one another, resulting in a diagonal-brace-free structure. Taking future relocation of the facility into consideration, the V-shaped joint was designed to achieve both simple assembling and dismantling, and aesthetics with a lighter appearance. The facility has been built for Tokyo Olympic and Paralympic Games in 2020 and its future operation is not yet decided.

6-9-1 Toyosu, Koto-ku, Tokyo
Architectural design: Yukiharu Takematsu+E.P.A
Structural design: KAP,Taiyo Kogyo Corporation
Construction: Chuo Construction co.,Ltd
Completion: 2016
Structure type: Roofing/Pillow-type ETFE cushion and Curved laminated wood structure, Beam/ Steel arch, Column/ Reinforcement concrete

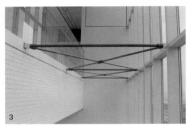

1 / Appearance of building

2 / On-site welded transom

3 / Mullions are connected to the internal reinforced concrete structures by horizontal braces to prevent buckling of a member and the entire frame. The horizontal members are less noticeable and do not disturb the pattern of the mullion's rectangular grid when looking into the building from a distance.

4–5 / The horizontal brace is loaded with compressive and tensile forces as the building is subjected to various loads and actions. The brace buckles against large compressive forces. Therefore, the brace end is joined to the frame with a coupler that can slide and does not transmit the force of contracting movement to the brace members.

Kasai Seaside Park Rest House

Fusion of architectural expression and structural system

Transparent architecture with floating roof

When you leave Kasairinkaikoen Station on the JR Keiyo Line and walk along a gentle slope of the stone pavement toward up to the sea, you will see a glass box architecture used as a rest house. Inside, there is an observation space where people can stroll around. The space is contained in a box made of glass and mullion of outer skin, and the roof looks as if it were floating above the space. This work is one of the pioneering works of transparent architecture, a trend in modern architecture.

The shape of the entire rest house is a simple rectangular with a height of 11 m, length of 74 m, and width of 6.6 m. There are reinforced concrete passages inside, and steel frames support the roof and the outer skin.

The structural members that play a dual role as the columns and mullion of the outer wall are made of Fire Resistant steel (FR steel), which was a new material at the time, and glass is attached directly to the structure with a batten. This detailed design contributes to its simple and compact appearance.

Invisible fittings made by machining

This building aims at architectural expression with high precision and smooth finish like a machine. Unlike ordinary buildings, the viewer cannot see or know where the joints are.

The horizontal transom members are welded to vertical mullions in a factory, and then a smooth machine-like finish is achieved by using an originally developed small machine tool and scraping the welded surface slightly into a rounded shape by craftsmen. Frames were manufactured at the factory every three spans with half-span length transom on both sides and transported to the site for on-site assembly.

Transoms of adjacent frames were welded on-site. Welding for jointing metal requires a large amount of heat, which may change the properties of the metals and cause unfavorable distortion. Therefore, for the connection of the transoms to the mullion, only the upper and lower parts of end cross section were welded with a small amount of welding that can resist the bending moment. In addition, since the transmitted force is smaller in the center region, the members were thinned to minimize the amount of welding and heat distortion.

6-2-3 Rinkaicho, Edogawa-ku, Tokyo
Architectural design: Taniguchi and Associates
Structural design: Araya Masato + Kimura Toshihiko and Associates
Construction: TOA & NAKAZATO CORPORATE joint venture
Completion: 1995
Structure type: Steel construction & Reinforced concrete construction

Alphabetical Index

Supervision

Ken'ichi Kawaguchi

The University of Tokyo

Born in Tokyo in 1962

Graduated from Waseda University 1985

Completed doctoral course at the University of Tokyo 1991

Lecturer, Institute of Industrial Science (IIS), the University of Tokyo 1991 Visiting scholar at Imperial College London and Cambridge University 1993 Associate Professor, IIS, the University of Tokyo 1996 Professor, IIS, the University of Tokyo 2006

Main structiral design works

Tension Truss Dome Annex on Building C (1991)

White Rhino I (2001)

Building No.2, the University of Tokyo (2005)

White Rhino II (2017)

Treatises/Research/Awards

1999 The Young Researcher Award of Architectural Institute of Japan

2004 The Best Paper Award from Membrane Structures Association of Japan

2008 The Japan Society of Seismic Isolation Award

2012 The AIJ Prize of Architectural Institute of Japan

2016 Honorary Professor of Tianjin University, China

2020 The Taisei Foundation, Gold Medal, 2020.

2021 Pioneers' Award, the University of Surrey

Book

"Morphological Analysis" (Second-author of double author, Bifukan Publishing Co., Ltd, 1991)

"All about architectures instructed by professionals" (Chief editor, Natsume-sha Co., Ltd, 2010)

"Generalized inverse and application to structural engineering"

(Single author, Corona Publishing Co., Ltd, 2011)

"Fifty Years of Progress for Shell and Spatial Structures" (Section 8.2: Cable Structures, Published by IASS, 2011)

Toru Takeuchi

Tokyo Institute of
Technology

Born in Osaka in 1960
Graduated from Tokyo Institute of Technology in 1984
(M. Eng.)
1984-2002 Nippon Steel corporation, Building Div.
1990-1992 Ove Arup London
2001 Dr. Eng. , Tokyo Institute of Technology
2003 Associate professor, Tokyo Institute of Technology
2009 Professor, Tokyo Institute of Technology

Main structural design works

The Center, Hong Kong (JSCA Awards 2000)
Tokyo Tech Midorigaoka-1st building retrofit
(Structural design award 2006)
Tokyo Tech Library
(BCJ Prize 2013, AIJ design commendation 2013)
Tokyo Tech Environmental Energy Innovation Building (Good
Design Award 2012, AIJ design commendation 2014)
Tokyo-Express Midorigaoka-station (2013)

Treatises/Research/Awards

Seismic performance of steel spatial structures with energy
dissipation members
(AIJ Prize / Research div. , 2011)

Book

"Damage mitigation technology for urban structures", (Asakura
publish, 2011)
"Mechanics / Material / Structural Design",
(Co-authored, Kenchiku-gijyutsu, 2012)
"Buckling-Restrained Braces and Applications",
(JSSI, AIJ Book Award 2017)
"Basic theory and design of shell and spatial structures"
(Co-authored, Kyoto University Press, 2019)
"Guide to Earthquake Response Evaluation of Metal Roof
Spatial Structures" (IASS WG8, 2019)

Writing cooperation

Taro Mizutani Taisei Corporation (P.14–15)

Osamu Hosozawa Shinozuka Research Institute (Former Taisei Corporation) (P.14–15)

Yasuhiko Asaoka Obayashi Corporation (P.16–17)

Hatsutaro Tanaka Shimizu Corporation (P.18–19)

Masahiro Hoshino Takenaka Corporation (P.20–21)

Yuuki Hamada Takenaka Corporation (P.20–21)

Ryunosuke Inoue Azusa Sekkei Co., Ltd. (P.26–27)

Chikara Konishi Kyoritsu Industries Co., Ltd. (P.26–27)

Photo and Drawing Credits

Japan National Stadium (P.14–15)
Photo1 & 2: JAPAN SPORT COUNCIL
Drawing: Taisei Corporation

TOKYO AQUATICS CENTER (P.16–17)
Photo & Drawing: Obayashi Corporation

Ariake Gymnastics Centre (P.18–19)
Photo1: SS., Ltd. Toshifumi Kato
Photo2 & 3: ken'ichi Suzuki
Drawing4–6: SHIMIZU CORPORATION

Ariake Arena (P.20–21)
Photo1 & 2 Miyagawa
Drawing3: Tokyo Metropolitan Home Page
Drawing4: Takenaka Corporation

Haneda Airport Terminal 2 (P.26–27)
Photo & Drawing: Azusa Sekkei Co., Ltd.

Haneda Airport Terminal 3 (P.28–29)
Photo1: Tokyo International Air Terminal
        Corporation
Photo2 & Drawing3: Azusa Sekkei Co., Ltd.

Tokyo Station Marunouchi Station Building
(P.36–37)
Photo1: PIXTA
Photo2–4: Kawaguchi Lab.The University of
        Tokyo
Photo5: East Japan Railway Company

Tokyo International Forum (P.38–39)
Photo1: SOGO-SHIKAKU Co., Ltd.
Drawing2: Takeuchi Lab.Tokyo Institute of
        Technology

Mitsubishi Ichigokan Museum (P.40–41)
Photo1 & 2: PIXTA
Photo3 & 4: SOGO-SHIKAKU Co., Ltd.

Maison Hermès (P.42–43)
Photo1: Shinkenchiku-sha
Drawing2: Arup

Nakagin Capsule Tower Building (P.44–45)
Photo1: Tomio Ohashi
Drawing2: Kisho Kurokawa architect &
        associates

**Shizuoka Press and Broadcasting Center
in Tokyo** (P.46–47)
Photo1: SOGO-SHIKAKU Co., Ltd.
Drawing2: Created based on materials
        provided by Tange Associates

MIKIMOTO Ginza 2 (P.48–49)
Photo1 &
Drawing2–3: Toyo Ito & Associates, Architects

Yoyogi National Stadium Gymnasiums
(P.58–61)
Photo1 & 2: PIXTA
Drawing &

Photo3–6 & 9–8: KAWAGUCHI & ENGINEERS
Photo7: JAPAN SPORT COUNCIL

TOD'S Omotesando (P.62–63)
Photo1: Nacasa & Partners Inc.
Photo & Drawing2: Toyo Ito & Associates,
                                    Architects

Prada Aoyama (P.64–65)
Photo1: Prada Japan
Drawing2 & Photo3: Takenaka Corporation

Museum cone (P.66–67)
Photo & Drawing1–3: Yoshinori Nito

The National Art center, Tokyo (P.68–69)
Photo1 & 3–5: Koji Kobayashi/SPIRAL
Drawing2: Nihon Sekkei, Inc.

Tokyo Tower (P.70–71)
Photo1 & 2: TOKYO TOWER Co., Ltd. &
                          Takenaka Corporation
Photo3 & 4: Takenaka Corporation

Tokyo Metropolitan Gymnasium (P.72)
Tokyo Sports Benefits Coporation

House of Tower (P.73)
Photo left: ©Osamu Murai
Photo right: MEHRDAD HADIGHI
Drawing: AZUMA ARCHITECT&ASSOCIATES

Tokyo Metropolitan Government Building
(P.80–81)
Photo1: PIXTA
Drawing2 & 3: Tokyo Metropolitan Government

Mode Gakuen Cocoon Tower (P.82)
Photo1: SOGO-SHIKAKU Co., Ltd.
Drawing2: Arup

NTT Docomo Yoyogi Building (P.83)
Photo1 & Drawing2:
Takeuchi Lab.Tokyo Institute of Technology

Tokyo Dome (P.88–89)
Photo1 & 2: Tokyo Dome
Photo3 & Blower: Takenaka Corporation
Drawing: Kawaguchi Lab.The University of
                Tokyo

St Mary's Cathedral (P.90–91)
Photo1–3: Sekiguchi Catholic Church

Drawing4 & 5: Tange Associates

**The National Museum of Western Art, Main
Building** (P.96–97)
Photo1: SOGO-SHIKAKU Co., Ltd.
Photo 2 & 4: Fondation Le Corbusier
Drawing3: ©F.L.C. / ADAGP, Paris & JASPAR,
                    Tokyo, 2021 C3613
Drawing5: Takeuchi Lab.Tokyo Institute of
                Technology

Tokyo Bunka Kaikan (P.98–99)
Photo1: Tokyo Bunka Kaikan
Drawing2 & 3: Reprinted from
"Toshihiko Kimura's Structural Philosophy"
(KAJIMA INSTITUTE PUBLISHING CO., LTD.)

**Tokyo National Museum Horyuji Treasures
Museum** (P.100–101)
Photo1: Tokyo National Museum
Drawing2: Yoshio Taniguchi and Associates

Tokyo skytree (P.104–107)
Photo1: Tobu Railway Co., Ltd. &
                Tobu Tower Skytree Co., Ltd. &
                Tobu Town Solamachi Co., Ltd.
Drawing2–6: Nikken Sekkei Ltd.

Edo-Tokyo Museum (P.108–109)
Photo1: Edo-Tokyo Museum
Photo2: Tokyo Metropolitan Government
Drawing3: SOGO-SHIKAKU Co., Ltd.

Sensoji Temple and Asakusa Towers
(P.110–111)
Photo1: PIXTA
Drawing2 & Photo3: Japan Open-air Folk
                                    House Museum
Photo4: Edo-Tokyo Museum

Bridge Cruise in Tokyo Bay & Sumida River
(P.112–123)
P.112
photo: PIXTA
P.113–115
Drawing: Kawaguchi Lab.The University of
                Tokyo
P.117–123
Photo 1 & 2: Tokyo Mizube Cruising Line
Photo3: The Kensetsutsushin Sinmbun
                Corporation
Photo4–16:Kawaguchi Lab.The University of
                Tokyo

Photo of Toyomi Bridge: SOGO-SHIKAKU Co.,Ltd.
Photo of Ukiyoe prints: TOKYO FUJI ART
　　　　　　　　　MUSEUM
Photo of Kokugikan: PIXTA
Photo of the first kokugikan & Photo of Ukiyoe
prints: EDO-TOKYO MUSEUM/DNPartcom

Tokyo Big Sight　(P.130–131)
Photo1: PIXTA
Photo3 & 4: AXS Satow Inc.
Photo5: Tokyo Big Sight
Drawing2: Created based on materials
　　　　　　provided by AXS Satow Inc.

**Fuji Television Headquarters Building
(FCG Building)**　(P.132)
Photo1: SOGO-SHIKAKU Co., Ltd.

Shin-toyosu Brillia Running Stadium　(P.133)
Photo1: Nacasa & Partners

Kasai Seaside Park Rest House
(P.134–135)
Photo1: Shinkenchiku-sha
Photo2–5: OAK Structual design office

Translation cooperation

The University of Tokyo　Kawaguchi Laboratory

Shoma Nagai

Shota Horiguchi

Tokyo Institute of Technology　Takeuchi Laboratory

Mykyta Kovalenko

Deepshikha Nair

Ben Sitler

Panumas Saingam

Fraze Craze Inc.

Map creation cooperation

Kazuya Naganuma

Yuki Mori

Authors of original Japanese version

Masato Araya　Deceased, Prof. Emeritus Waseda University

Hiroaki Harada　Nikken Sekkei Ltd.

Hirofumi Ohno　Ohno Japan

Ken'ichi Kawaguchi　The University of Tokyo

Mitsuhiro Kanada　Tokyo University of Arts

Noriaki Yamada　Yamada Noriaki Structural Design Office

Toru Takeuchi　Tokyo Institute of Technology

STRUCTURAL DESIGN MAP TOKYO

First Edition: September 25, 2021 (First Printing)

Supervision: Ken'ichi Kawaguchi, Toru Takeuchi

Publisher: Takashi Kishi
SOGO-SHIKAKU Co., Ltd.
22F SHINJUKU NOMURA BLDG. 1-26-2
Nishishinjuku, Shinjuku-ku, Tokyo, 163-0557 JAPAN
Mail: books@shikaku.co.jp

Edition: SOGO-SHIKAKU Co., Ltd. Publishing Department
(Yoshiki Arakaki, Sakae Kobayashi, Tomoko Matsuda)

SOGO-SHIKAKU Co., Ltd. (Takehisa Nakashiro)

Design: SOGO-SHIKAKU Co., Ltd. Publishing Department (Rin Shida)

Cover Illustration: Yoshifumi Takeda

Map: Fromage

Printing: Shinano Co., Ltd.

Printed in Japan

ISBN 978-4-86417-403-9

Give the people who make the city the power to draw the future

We are the school which continuing to produce the largest first-class architectures in Japan.
The SOGO-SHIKAKU GAKUIN Philosophy is contributing to society with fostering of superior human resources.

Others

56.9%
Japanese who got the first-class registered architect in 2016–2020 have student at SOGO-SHIKAKU GAKUIN.

SOGO-SHIKAKU-GAKUIN